ORTHO'S All About
Bonsai

Written by
Penelope O'Sullivan

Meredith® Books
Des Moines, Iowa

Ortho's All About Bonsai
Editor: Denny Schrock
Senior Associate Design Director: Tom Wegner
Assistant Editor: Harijs Priekulis
Copy Chief: Terri Fredrickson
Copy and Production Editor: Victoria Forlini
Photographers: Marty Baldwin, Jay Wilde
Editorial Operations Manager: Karen Schirm
Managers, Book Production: Pam Kvitne,
    Marjorie J. Schenkelberg, Rick von Holdt
Contributing Copy Editor: Lorraine Ferrell
Technical Consultants: Ron Heinen, Chase Rosade
Contributing Proofreaders: Ellen Bingham, Julie Cahalan,
    Sara Henderson
Contributing Map Illustrator: Jana Fothergill
Contributing Prop/Photo Stylists: Susan Strelecki,
    Diane Witosky
Indexer: Kathleen Poole
Editorial and Design Assistants: Kathleen Stevens,
    Karen McFadden

**Additional Editorial Contributions from
    Art Rep Services**
Director: Chip Nadeau
Designer: lk Design
Illustrator: Dave Brandon

Meredith® Books
Editor in Chief: Linda Raglan Cunningham
Design Director: Matt Strelecki
Executive Editor, Gardening and Home Improvement:
    Benjamin W. Allen
Executive Editor, Gardening: Michael McKinley

Publisher: James D. Blume
Executive Director, Marketing: Jeffrey Myers
Executive Director, New Business Development:
    Todd M. Davis
Executive Director, Sales: Ken Zagor
Director, Operations: George A. Susral
Director, Production: Douglas M. Johnston
Business Director: Jim Leonard

Vice President and General Manager: Douglas J. Guendel

Meredith Publishing Group
President, Publishing Group: Stephen M. Lacy
Vice President-Publishing Director: Bob Mate

Meredith Corporation
Chairman and Chief Executive Officer: William T. Kerr

In Memoriam: E.T. Meredith III (1933–2003)

Note to the Readers: Due to differing conditions, tools, and individual skills, Meredith Corporation assumes no responsibility for any damages, injuries suffered, or losses incurred as a result of following the information published in this book. Before beginning any project, review the instructions carefully, and if any doubts or questions remain, consult local experts or authorities. Because codes and regulations vary greatly, you always should check with authorities to ensure that your project complies with all applicable local codes and regulations. Always read and observe all of the safety precautions provided by manufacturers of any tools, equipment, or supplies, and follow all accepted safety procedures.

Thanks to
Janet Anderson, DaSu Bonsai Studio, Mary Irene Swartz

Photographers
(Photographers credited may retain copyright ©
to the listed photographs.)
L = Left, R = Right, C = Center, B = Bottom, T = Top

William C. Aplin: 5B; **Brussel's Bonsai Nursery:** 13TR, 18B, 47TL, 76R, 86, 87B, 88, 96, 107; **Eric Crichton/ Garden Picture Library:** 75; **Tommy Dodson/Unicorn Stock Photos:** 68B; **Jim Doyle/Nature's Way Nursery:** 92, 109, 117; **John Edwards/Mike Page:** 100; **Catriona Tudor Erler:** 28TR, 28CTL, 35TR, 44BL, 54T, 81, 87T, 91, 94L, 101; **Derek Fell:** 12TR, 13BR, 17T, 21BL, 46BL, 48BL, 71, 77, 85BR, 103T, 112, 120; **John Glover:** 19T, 123; **Golden State Bonsai Collection North/Michael S. Thompson:** 89, 111, 116; **Anne Gordon Images:** 14B; **Jessie M. Harris:** 69, 73, 83, 110; **Lynne Harrison:** 12TL, 13CL, 99, 103B; **Saxon Holt:** 7BL; **Jerry Howard/Positive Images:** 14T, 64T; **Jacqui Hurst/Garden Picture Library:** 9B, 17C, 20B, 70, 85TR, 90; **Bill Johnson:** 8T, 14C, 16C, 16B, 19C, 35BL, 76BL, 84, 93, 98, 106, 113, 118; **Rosemary Kautzky:** 114; **Robert Klei/Jiusan Bonsai Studio:** 19B, 45; **Marilynn McAra:** 3B, 7TL, 7BR, 12B, 13BL, 23C, 23R, 28TL, 29BR, 30, 31, 32, 46TL, 80T; **Alan Mitchell/Garden Picture Library:** 46BR; **John Neubauer/Garden Picture Library:** 82, 104; **Clive Nichols/World of Koi, Chelsea:** 20TL; **Jerry Pavia:** 5T, 8B, 10, 11, 16T, 18T, 49T, 50, 102, 121; **Ann Reilly/Positive Images:** 95; **Howard Rice/Garden Picture Library:** 80B; **Richard Shiell:** 17B, 33Row2#1; **J. S. Sira/ Garden Picture Library:** 105; **Friedrich Strauss/Garden Picture Library:** 7TR; **Michael S. Thompson:** 4, 13CR, 15T, 15CL, 15B, 18C, 39, 47BR, 54B, 61T, 66T, 68T, 72, 74, 79, 94R, 97, 115; **Mark Turner:** 3T, 9T, 20TR, 23L, 36TL, 47TR, 48BR, 52B, 60, 65T; **Mark Turner/Elandan Gardens:** 6, 15CR, 34BR, 47BL; **Michel Viard/Garden Picture Library:** 85BL; **Perry Welling:** 21BR, 52T; **Rick Wetherbee:** 13TL, 22, 25TL, 25TR, 25CT, 27BR, 28CT, 35BR, 38, 53, 55TL, 55TR, 58B, 59B, 78, 108, 119; **Weyerhaeuser Company, Pacific Rim Bonsai Collection:** 76TL

On the cover: Alan & Linda Detrick

All of us at Meredith® Books are dedicated to providing you with the information and ideas you need to enhance your home and garden. We welcome your comments and suggestions about this book. Write to us at:
    Meredith Corporation
    Meredith Gardening Books
    1716 Locust St.
    Des Moines, IA 50309–3023

If you would like to purchase any of our gardening, home improvement, cooking, crafts, or home decorating and design books, check wherever quality books are sold. Or visit us at: meredithbooks.com

If you would like more information on other Ortho products, call 800/225-2883 or visit us at: www.ortho.com

Bonsai for Every Home

The classic bonsai is a tree or shrub grown in a shallow container and trained or pruned to create an artistic effect resembling a full-size plant from nature.

No matter the size of your home, there's always space for bonsai. These miniaturized trees and shrubs add charm and individuality to rooms as well as decks, balconies, or patios if your climate supports the plants.

Bonsai (BOHN-seye) consists of a stylized tree grown in a soil-filled shallow container and pruned to create the illusion of a mature or ancient tree. In fact, *bonsai* means "tree in a container." A potted tree differs from a bonsai, which is shaped to follow specific patterns of growth and to exaggerate the appearance of old age. With careful pruning, bonsai trees and shrubs develop gnarly roots, thick flared or twisted trunks, and distressed bark. Caring for bonsai can be as simple as nurturing a houseplant or as challenging as maintaining a miniature landscape on a granite slab.

Growing bonsai will delight you, no matter what your level of gardening expertise. With patience, some tools, and this how-to guide to traditional forms and practices, you can start cultivating bonsai today.

Benefits of Bonsai

Bonsai bring diverse forms of enjoyment to those who grow them. Following are some of the reasons to grow bonsai:

1. SELF-EXPRESSION: Bonsai is an art form. It offers the same enjoyment as painting a picture or designing a flower garden. Guidelines exist, but it is your choice to follow them or try something different. You are the creator.

2. QUALITY OF LIFE: Ask gardeners why they enjoy gardening, and you will likely hear about the satisfaction of growing healthy plants and watching them change over time. Nurturing a living object may satisfy your need to give to something outside yourself.

3. SERENITY: The same inner peace that you experience on a long outdoor hike can be yours without leaving home, because bonsai is nature's theater in miniature. Contemplating nature by studying your bonsai, which represents the natural world self-contained and idealized, will bring moments of awe and a feeling of peace.

4. SOCIAL LIFE: Thousands of people around the world share your interest in bonsai. Clubs abound in North America, on the Internet, and abroad, bringing diverse people together for meetings and shows. Linked by their passion for the art and skill of bonsai, these enthusiasts provide their peers with information on growing and caring for bonsai.

5. CONNECTION WITH THE PAST: People have experimented with bonsai making for 2,000 years. Through the ages, techniques for pruning and shaping bonsai evolved, along with guidelines for the naturalistic or exaggerated styling of plants. Adapting these styles and techniques to your own ideas and methods ties you into the timeline of bonsai history and connects you with bonsai artists, enthusiasts, and growers of the past.

6. LONG LIFE: As long as you care for your bonsai, it will thrive. Some trees in nature survive for hundreds of years. Bonsai trees may live even longer; some 1,000-year-old specimens are in existence. Bonsai trees can endure beyond a human lifetime, often passing from generation to generation in a family and representing the combined creative essence of those who have created and cared for it.

7. HOUSEHOLD DECOR: Because of its sculptural traits, bonsai can enhance your living space. The plant's striking lines, harmonious balance, and depiction of nature make it a focal point in indoor or outdoor rooms. Although not every bonsai can live indoors, some species will thrive in the dim light and dry atmosphere of your house or apartment.

8. SIZE: Bonsai techniques keep trees and shrubs from achieving their natural size. Ginkgos in nature can reach 100 feet tall. The same tree grown as bonsai may reach up to 3 feet, but only after many, many years. The small size of a bonsai makes it easier to move and display in limited space than a mature potted tree growing in a large decorative pot or container.

9. MULTISEASONAL INTEREST: Just as you watch the seasons come and go in the landscape outside your home, you can watch the seasons change by observing your bonsai go through its yearly cycles of growth and dormancy.

10. SPECIAL EFFECTS: With special pruning, a crab apple bonsai can produce several extra-large fruits, adding bright color and drama to your plant. Other glories of bonsai include spring flowers on a cherry tree, fall color on a Japanese maple, and the smooth matte bark of a beech tree in winter.

Growing bonsai is a rewarding hobby that combines artistry and gardening.

Why This Particular Bonsai Book?

Because of bonsai's growing popularity, the number of books on the subject is also growing. *Ortho's All About Bonsai,* however, is written specifically for bonsai beginners and enthusiasts in North America. You can find the tools, resources, and tree and shrub varieties described in this book in North America. Both common and botanical plant names and spellings are those frequently used by American nurseries and growers.

Over time, bonsai techniques can transform a young plant into an ancient-looking, weathered tree.

How to use this book

Begin to explore bonsai by skimming *Ortho's All About Bonsai* from cover to cover. This book brings together detailed bonsai-related charts, illustrations and photographs as well as clearly written text. Each chapter begins with a short description of the material being introduced, so you know the chapter's content in advance. Refer to the index on page 126 when you need a question answered. For detailed advice, join a bonsai society to support your efforts. Bonsai resources and organizations are listed in the Resources pages at the end of the book.

Secrets of successful bonsai

No matter how busy you are, take the time to learn the secrets of successful bonsai. Once you've mastered these tips, growing bonsai will be easy and fun.

KNOW WHAT YOU WANT. What is your reason for growing bonsai? Would you like a new type of houseplant, a decoration, or a hardy tree that spends most of its life outdoors? Certain plants require more maintenance than others. Do you have time for a high-maintenance plant or would you prefer one that is easier to keep? Answer these questions and you are on the way to choosing a bonsai that matches your sense of beauty and your way of life.

THINK AHEAD. Consider which bonsai style appeals to you and how you can best achieve it. For instance, before you start pruning, understand the look you want to accomplish. It will affect each pinch and cut you make, so think about your tree and the desired results before you begin to shape it.

GROW THE RIGHT PLANT FOR THE PLACE. Keeping your bonsai healthy is easy when you choose a plant that suits your climate. Cultivate trees like pine, spruce, oaks, and elms outside. They need cold-winter dormancy to maintain their vigor. In extreme cold, protect them from the effects of frost and icy wind. Unless

you live in a frost-free climate, bring tropical and subtropical plants indoors when night temperatures consistently drop below 50°F.

CHOOSE A HEALTHY PLANT.
Select sturdy injury-free plant material for bonsai. Before buying bonsai, check plants for pests and signs of neglect or disease. These include broken branches; a powdery coating on foliage; or dead, wilted, spotty, and discolored leaves or stems.

MAINTAIN REGULARLY.
Because a bonsai lives in a shallow pot, it needs more frequent attention than a tree growing in garden soil outdoors. Appropriate potting soil, adequate water, and sufficient fertilizer during the growing period will make your bonsai thrive. Timely pruning and shaping will give it the form you desire. Observe your bonsai daily, even if it doesn't need care.

TREAT PROBLEMS WHEN THEY ARE SMALL. Although most bonsai remain healthy, some develop problems. Ensure your bonsai's vigor by noting changes when you water the plant or perform routine upkeep. If you see any signs of disease or pest infestation, deal with them immediately. If you have someone care for your bonsai while you are away from home, make sure you explain how and when to water it.

SELECT THE RIGHT CONTAINER. A bonsai container is not only functional; it is also part of a harmonious composition made up of plant and pot. The container's form and color complement the style and size of the tree, while the location of the tree in the pot balances the overall design.

In early summer, medium-green leaves cover crabapple branches.

In spring, crabapples produce pink or white, often fragrant blooms.

Bonsai containers are typically made of glazed or unglazed, earth-tone ceramic and may be handmade or machined.

READ, READ, READ. The more you read about bonsai and the more bonsai pictures you see, the better your idea of how a bonsai should look and grow. Good design sense is not innate. It develops from repeated exposure to well-designed trees with poor examples for contrast. Even better than reading books is studying actual bonsai. Some

public bonsai collections are listed on page 125. Many communities have bonsai shows you can attend to see good examples of the art.

ENJOY THE PROCESS. The pleasure of bonsai draws as much from the process of creating it as it does from admiring the result. Since many bonsai develop slowly, you may become attuned to small changes in your tree—a thickening trunk or the effect of repotting and pruning on the vigor of an aged plant.

Some crabapples hold fruits for months.

Branch patterns create winter interest.

Bonsai Panorama

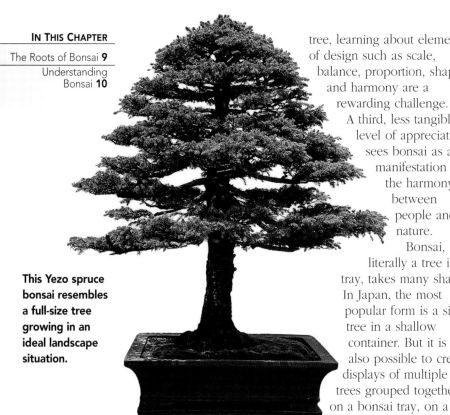

This Yezo spruce bonsai resembles a full-size tree growing in an ideal landscape situation.

The art of bonsai is a product of ancient Asian cultures that produced and perfected it. Bonsai art imitates nature. Even when Chinese and Japanese practices vary, they produce bonsai that evoke a deep response from viewers. By studying the work of bonsai masters and practicing the horticultural skills described in this book, you will develop a knack for bonsai and the ability to impart a flair all your own.

Bonsai art

Bonsai imitates nature on a compact, three-dimensional scale. While most people readily acquire the techniques needed to miniaturize a potted tree, learning about elements of design such as scale, balance, proportion, shape, and harmony are a rewarding challenge.

A third, less tangible level of appreciation sees bonsai as a manifestation of the harmony between people and nature.

Bonsai, literally a tree in a tray, takes many shapes. In Japan, the most popular form is a single tree in a shallow container. But it is also possible to create displays of multiple trees grouped together on a bonsai tray, on a rock slab, or in a low pot. Tree groups consist of several trunks emerging from the same roots or a group of individual plants. These bonsai groups evoke images of the natural world that may range from several twisting, windswept trees to an island of trees in an open landscape or a forest of fine, straight-trunk trees reaching for light.

On a more detailed scale, a style known as *saikei,* or tray landscape, represents entire scenes from nature. Displayed with carefully chosen trees, shrubs, rocks, and mosses, these bonsai are literal views from nature. Rocks represent mountains; sand simulates water; moss, gravel, and other groundcovers carpet the earth; and trees and shrubs grow from rocky nooks, their roots clinging to the contours of the jagged stone.

In addition to naturalistic bonsai, a less common type consists of a tree contorted for art's sake. Divorced from natural growth patterns, these distortions in trunk and branches look like intellectual exercises or bizarre objects of the imagination.

Group plantings often include rocks and mosses to imitate scenes from nature.

The Roots of Bonsai

The art of growing trees in pots probably started in India. It spread to China as an imperial pastime about 2,000 years ago and gained acceptance among the nobility, who grew their trees in shallow, decorative pots or in landscaped trays that imitated detailed natural scenes. Soon miniature versions of artificial rock gardens complete with trees, rocks, rivers, houses, animals, and people became fashionable.

During the T'ang Dynasty (618–907 A.D.), bonsai enthusiasts came from all levels of Chinese society and carried their hobby to Japan. By 1200 A.D., Chinese writers and scholars had produced many books on growing and caring for bonsai. Chinese styles comprised the basis for Japanese bonsai, which refined the art. The Japanese made protocols for styling and cultivating bonsai. Although Japanese growers introduced bonsai to Europeans on a large scale at the 1878 Paris World Fair, bonsai did not take off as a widespread hobby in North America until after World War II.

In nature, a tough tree may take root in a soil pocket on a barren mountainside.

In bonsai, rocks become mountains, and a water tray forms a lake from which the mountains emerge. Trees grow on the rocks in soil-filled crevices.

Understanding Bonsai

Because of the growing popularity of bonsai, you should know what to look for when evaluating the trees. First, determine if the growers have used suitable styles for their chosen bonsai species; then note how effectively the tree follows the style's basic guidelines. Each species has distinctive characteristics. It is the grower's job to accentuate those traits, thus creating an enhanced image of nature.

Tree roots on a well-made bonsai are usually prominent and expansive. They radiate in all directions, giving strength and stability to the composition. The trunk rises from the roots, thick at the base and narrowing toward the treetop. Any trunk shaped into curves or angles should look artless. Pruning to thicken the trunk makes the tree look older, a valuable trait in most bonsai, but the thickness of the trunk should be proportionate to the size of the tree.

Branches also taper from bases to tips, and their lengths are in proportion to trunk size. No branch should sit opposite, nor parallel, another. Branches should be staggered at different heights around the tree, with no branch overlapping another when seen from above. Except for broom-style bonsai or the top third of other styles, branches grow to the sides and back, not toward the front. That is because it is important to see as much of the branch and trunk structure as possible. Since branches do not grow that way naturally, you must prune and train them to achieve the appropriate form. Handle branches carefully because the best bonsai show no cuts. Like the branches, foliage size fits the scale of the trunk and branches; thus, leaves should look healthy but small compared to those same leaves on a larger plant.

At first glance, differences between Chinese and Japanese bonsai are slight. Chinese bonsai may be bigger, ranging up to 5 feet tall, whereas Japanese bonsai is typically less than 3 feet tall. Japanese bonsai growers heighten a tree's natural form, accentuating the trunk's taper, while the trunks on Chinese bonsai trees may have less flare. Similarly, both roots and branches on Chinese bonsai may be more slender than on Japanese trees. The Chinese use decorative containers of materials like fine painted porcelain. These pots are sometimes larger and deeper than those of the Japanese and are more important to the overall aesthetics.

Chinese trees may show less taper and leaner roots and limbs than Japanese bonsai.

Classic Japanese bonsai display a tapered trunk, spreading roots, and a balanced arrangement of branches.

THE BEST
Bonsai for You

**Grown outdoors,
hardy conifers
make fine bonsai
in temperate
climates.**

Hardy deciduous trees like
maples and hornbeams must live
outdoors to stay healthy.

**Littleleaf
cotoneaster is an
excellent choice
for growers of
tiny *mame* bonsai.**

It is time to discover which bonsai best fits your tastes, your interests, and your lifestyle. By looking at the differences between indoor and outdoor bonsai and exploring the range of plants available, you can choose which bonsai to grow. Bonsai styles are as important as the species because not every plant species is suited to each style. In nature, trees occur in different environments and grow in unique ways. Bonsai artists seek to reproduce these effects. Over the centuries, growers developed styles to express and refine the habits of trees in their natural settings. This chapter covers bonsai styles and discusses how to display your bonsai in a house or garden setting.

Choosing the right bonsai

OUTDOOR BONSAI: If you think bonsai are houseplants, you are not alone. Yet most bonsai cannot live indoors. They are hardy trees that go dormant in cold weather and revive the following spring. Conifers such as pine, spruce, and hemlock and deciduous trees such as maples, oaks, and elms must live outdoors to stay healthy. Likewise, flowering quince, shrubby cinquefoil, some azaleas, and other woody bonsai shrubs grow best when exposed to the cold. If you decide to grow these plants, you may have to water them daily in summer and protect their

shallow-potted roots from harsh winter winds.

TROPICAL AND SUBTROPICAL: If you live where temperatures stay warm, then tropical and subtropical plants would make good bonsai subjects for you. In cold climates, these bonsai make good houseplants, although they can grow outdoors all summer in the North. Tropical and subtropical plants for bonsai include bougainvillea, camellia, fig, gardenia, serissa, and umbrella tree. These plants are also appropriate for apartment dwellers lacking a patio, balcony, or other outdoor space.

SUCCULENT: Proper pruning helps turn fleshy-leafed succulent plants into effective indoor bonsai. Jade plant, for example, is low maintenance and easy to grow. It can thrive indoors on a south-facing windowsill in glaring sunlight. It doesn't need much watering since it carries its own fluid supply in its leaves.

EVERGREEN: The Japanese put most evergreens into the *shohaku* bonsai group, a category that includes the classic pine bonsai. Some bonsai masters spend a lifetime trying to perfect this centuries-old favorite with its upright tapered trunk, well-composed branching pattern, and aged yet natural look. Other customary bonsai conifers include Yezo spruce, black pine, red pine, Sargent juniper, and Japanese yew.

DECIDUOUS: Deciduous trees that drop their leaves in autumn make excellent bonsai specimens since you can see time pass in the tree's changing looks. You can choose deciduous trees for many reasons—spring or summer flowers, colorful edible fruit, and brilliant fall color. Spring flowering trees and shrubs, including crabapple *(Malus)* and hawthorn *(Crataegus),* make superb bonsai subjects not only for the beauty of their flowers but in some instances for their sweet fragrance, bright fruit display, and intense fall color. Trees that do not belong to the traditional *shohaku* bonsai group, including most deciduous trees, are in the *zoki* bonsai group.

Sizes of bonsai

Most bonsai range from 6 to 36 inches high. Medium-size or *classical* trees 6 inches to 2 feet tall are widespread because one person can usually lift and maintain them with ease. Large or *imperial* bonsai range from 2 to 4 feet tall. Bonsai smaller than 12 inches make attractive table decorations in houses and apartments although the

plants that can be grown depend upon the climate indoors. Miniature bonsai, or *mame* bonsai, stand 2 to 6 inches tall. They are often

displayed in groups on shelves, where arrangement of the plants and their containers is as important as the plants.

Jade plant, a succulent, makes an easy indoor bonsai subject.

Fall to spring flowers and glossy leaves make camellia, a broadleaf evergreen, an appealing bonsai choice.

The pear tree has white spring blooms and lustrous green leaves.

This sweetheart ivy bonsai can grow indoors or outside with protection to Zone 7.

The fruits of 'Orange Glow' firethorn may last into winter.

Most Japanese cutleaf maples have outstanding fall color that persists into November.

Bonsai Styles and Motifs

Chokkan
CHOH-kahn

STRAIGHT TRUNK

An erect tapering trunk indicates the formal-upright or straight-trunk style.

Sometimes known as formal-upright, this style is based upon an ideal: a healthy, well-nourished tree growing in an open field without crowding, deprivation, or severe weather. In this benign environment, a tree would develop an upright trunk and a balanced crown. The trunk, rising from large roots that spread in every direction, tapers from the base to the crown and is free from visible pruning wounds. This basic style has a front and back view. Branches taper from trunk to tip and emerge from the trunk's sides and back, starting about one-third the height of the tree from the base. No branch grows opposite another. Since the branches decrease in length as they go up the tree, they form a triangle with fairly even sides. Straight-trunk bonsai exude a feeling of grandeur and permanence. Suitable for this style are evergreens such as Japanese white pine (*P. parviflora*) and Japanese black pine (*P. thunbergii*), juniper (*Juniperus*), hinoki false cypress (*Chamaecyparis obtusa*), and hemlock (*Tsuga*). Appropriate deciduous trees include gingko, beech (*Fagus*), zelkova, and larch (*Larix*).

Myo-gi
Mee-OH-gee

CURVED TRUNK

A tapering trunk with decreasing curves marks the curved-trunk style.

This popular style, also described as informal-upright, has a trunk with flowing curves that decrease in size near the crown. Wide-spreading roots (*nebari*) form a substantial base for a tapering trunk that, despite its gently winding form, is upright for the most part. From the front, you can see the trunk's main curve near the base slope to the left or to the right. Trees trained in the curved-trunk style are graceful to behold, even when their trunks are old and broad. The crown of an informal-upright tree may be fuller and have more branches than a formal-upright tree; but these branches, which typically form a triangle, still need careful positioning to balance the tree's gentle curves. This situation is evident in nature when a tree rises from a hillside or curves around to reach for daylight. The trunk is forced to bend in one direction and then arc back in the other direction to restore the balance. The curved-trunk or informal-upright style suits most evergreen and deciduous trees and shrubs, including pine (*Pinus*), spruce (*Picea*), cherry (*Prunus*), and azalea (*Rhododendron*).

Shakan
SHAH-kahn

SLANTING

Slanting style trees look dramatic yet stable, with branches uniformly arranged on the trunk.

Trees in the slanting style grow straight toward the crown but at a sloping angle. This single-trunk style evokes a natural tree that is leaning or toppling as the result of strong winds or a storm. Slanting may also occur when a tree grows tilted to reach daylight and then grows straight up to the sun once it's in the light. To balance the trunk's extreme slant and help fix the tree in the soil, the roots on the side opposite the slope grow longer and more plentiful than the dense, compact mass of roots directly under the trunk. The result is a tree that looks secure and permanent in spite of a precarious past. In the slanting style, the entire trunk does not have to be in line with the top of the tree, but usually the lower two-thirds of the trunk is straight or gently curved. The tree spreads high on the trunk with branches growing in every direction. This tree has few branches, which keeps it from looking top-heavy and ready to fall. Pines (*Pinus*), junipers (*Juniperus*), and larches (*Larix*) work well in the slanting style.

Fukinagashi
foo-kee-NAH-gah-shee

WINDSWEPT

This style captures the essence of a tree whipped by strong winds on a mountain peak. The trunk is usually slanted or curved, while the branches and twigs grow in the same direction, unable to resist the persistent pounding of the wind. Pines and junipers are well suited to this style, which can also be applied to deciduous trees. Multi-trunk trees trained in the windswept style increase the effect of this natural drama. To reinforce the desolate feeling of a mountaintop, you can grow windswept trees on slabs of rock instead of in dishes.

In nature, a windswept tree survives against the odds, embodying the invincible character of the human race.

Kengai and han-kengai
ken-GUY and HAHN-ken-guy

CASCADE & SEMI-CASCADE

Cascade-style bonsai symbolizes a tree surviving on a steep bank or overhanging rock face. Subjected to blizzards and storms, the tree is suspended above an abyss, stretching its branches out for light yet pulled down by its own weight. Technically, the trunk and branches of a cascade grow below the bottom of the bonsai dish. Cascade pots are small at the rim but deep to balance the plunging form of the tree. Semi-cascade bonsai looks more horizontal than a cascade. The tree's crown rises above the container's rim, while its trunk bends and its branches grow low and horizontal, dropping down no further than the bottom of the bowl. The pot of a semi-cascade bonsai is shallower than that of a cascade, since the depth of the container must stay proportionate to the fall of the tree.

Below: The crown of this hemlock semi-cascade rises above the rim of the dish.

Above: A deep pot stabilizes a cascade.

Bunjin-gi
Boon-JIN-gee

LITERATI

The elegance of the literati style comes from its elongated trunk and the airiness of its short branches only at the top of the plant. Literati were the Japanese artists and writers of the 18th and 19th centuries who admired all things Chinese, including their art and philosophy. Chinese scroll paintings may have influenced the development of literati-style bonsai in Japan. In nature, literati-type trees sometimes grow along Japanese roadsides where there is little natural light or at the seacoast. The wind makes them lean, and they drop their bottom branches. Bonsai growers strip down literati-style trees to their essentials, creating a feeling of lightness and austerity. The thin trunk grows at a graceful but irregular slant, and the meager branches have a delicate appearance. The relationship of the pot to the tree adds to the style's sophistication. Literati pots tend to be small, balancing the size of the container with the delicacy of the tree. Traditionally, literati bonsai are made from juniper, spruce, and pine.

The pot's small size and convex shape enhance a literati juniper's elegant lines.

Bonsai Styles and Motifs
(continued)

Ikadabuki
Ee-kah-DAH-boo-kee

In the raft style, a large tree dwarfs other minor trees grown from the same base.

RAFT

This style has a long raftlike base from which several trunks grow side by side. Raft-style bonsai imitates a landscape tree knocked over by harsh winds or a snowstorm. The tree trunk, now horizontal on the ground, begins to make roots where it touches the soil, and some of its branches become new trunks. To create a raft-style bonsai, the grower lays a live trunk or limb on soil. In the spots where the trunk meets the soil, new roots form and may eventually mingle with old roots, making for interesting twists and turns. A line of shoots emerges from the top of the horizontal trunk. This line of new growth becomes a row of little tree trunks as it matures. An experienced bonsai artist varies the gaps between trunks along with their height and width. If growers dislike planting in one straight row, they can add depth to certain designs by letting shoots grow from a subordinate branch of the main horizontal trunk or limb. Because a raft-style bonsai is usually long and narrow, it best fits an oval or rectangular dish.

Hokidachi
Hoh-KEE-dah-chee

BROOM

The broom style calls to mind the formal upright style with a trunk perpendicular to the ground, a radiating root base, and a triangular top. Instead of rising to a sharp point, however, the canopy of a *hokidachi* bonsai looks twiggy and somewhat rounded like the head of a broom. In nature, broom-shaped trees occur on flat open expanses of land where few trees obstruct the sunlight or compete for soil nutrients. The broom style is therefore best suited to deciduous plains trees with a vigorous erect habit of growth such as ginkgos, Japanese gray-bark elms *(Zelkova serrata),* and Japanese maple *(Acer palmatum).* With pruning, broom-style trees form dense yet finely branched canopies that fan out over a straight trunk. Broom style has year-round appeal. In leaf its balance is perfect and symmetrical. Yet after the leaves drop, you can see the intricate network of twigs and branches (ramification) that make this style so alluring.

Zelkovas have upthrust trunks that lend themselves to the erect broom style.

Sokan
SOH-kahn

TWIN TRUNK

The image of a parent and child inspires the twin-trunk bonsai style. Mothers and daughters and fathers and sons share a connection—they emerge from the same roots. But adults protect their children when they are young and keep them close. In nature, a tree with two trunks sometimes occurs when the main trunk of a tree divides at or just above root level, which can happen when a tree has been cut down and two trunks sprout from the original stump or when a low branch becomes a second trunk. To maintain the parent/child symbolism and boost the bonsai's visual appeal, the two trunks are not identical. Instead, there is a main trunk and a smaller trunk. The main trunk is the more upright, while the shorter, thinner trunk leans out at a slight angle. Twin trunks may be either curved or straight. When you look at a twin-trunk bonsai, you should see a unified tree with branches that, although separate and emerging from two trunks, fit together to form a coherent canopy when viewed from the front.

Seen together, the outer branches of each trunk form a triangle.

TRIPLE TRUNK

Sankan
SAHN-kahn

Similar to the twin-trunk style, a triple-trunk bonsai has three trunks of varying heights and thicknesses. Trunks usually emerge at root level or, in some instances, the third trunk grows out of one of the two main trunks. Whether you place the main trunk at the left, right, or center of the composition is up to you, but take care to keep the design balanced whichever you decide. Multi-trunk trees can stand upright with straight trunks; bend like windswept trees; or have the bare, ascetic, stretched-out form of literati-type bonsai. The positioning of foliage masses is key to giving a triple-trunk bonsai a balanced and unified look. The outer branches of the three trunks often form a tipped triangle. The uppermost angle stands for God, the middle is humanity, and the bottom corner represents the earth, the dwelling place of the human race.

Multiple trunks emphasize this interesting directional design.

FIVE TRUNK

Gokan
GOH-kahn

In the five-trunk style, five trees grow from one root system or by layering, a method for making new trees from parent trees by promoting new root growth along the trunk or branches of the original tree. The five trunks of this bonsai emerge at root level and differ in height and width. Seen from the front, one trunk does not cross another trunk, and all trunks are clearly visible. The branches of the group are unified and usually make a triangle. In nature, some deciduous trees such as birches and maples grow with multiple trunks. Conifers usually do not grow with five trunks. They, however, can look natural if they are arranged like a cluster of related trees in the woods. Making a bonsai with five trunks—each showing the effect of extreme weather—increases the impact of the weathering.

This five-trunk spruce bonsai resembles a naturally occurring stand of trees in an old abandoned field.

CLUMP

Kabudachi
ka-boo-DAH-chee

This style brings to mind a copse with several trunks subjected to the same environmental conditions. A clump-style bonsai has more than 5 trunks sprouting from one root system as near as possible to the soil or created by layering. For design purposes, create seven or nine trunks, since an uneven number of trunks looks better than an even number. The clump comprises two main trunks, a dominant and a lesser trunk, with minor trunks grouped around them. All trunks are visible from the front of the bonsai. Because trees in a clump derive from the same roots, they share the same visual details such as leaf size and bark character, adding to bonsai's unity. Try basing the overall design on a triangle to control the various elements and keep the design clean and cohesive.

'Foemina' Chinese juniper in the clump style looks like a miniature natural forest with many discernible trunks.

Bonsai Styles and Motifs
(continued)

Netsuranari
Nayt-SOO-rah-nah-ree

SINUOUS OR ROOT-LINKED

In the sinuous style, a tree produces other lesser trees at random from its roots. In nature, this happens when a branch bends and touches the soil, making roots at the contact point. From these new roots, a fresh shoot will arise that becomes a new tree. Several branches on one plant can layer or propagate themselves in more than one place, giving rise to

Each trunk, rising from the same roots, has identical leaves and varies in height and width.

several new root-linked trees. A root-linked planting may also develop through suckering. Some woody plants send up shoots or suckers along their surface roots. Again, these shoots become new trees or shrubs that form a colony around the parent plant. A successful sinuous-style planting looks like a natural grove with trunks that differ in spacing and dimension but are still part of a unified whole. Among the plants suited to this style are five-needle pine, needle juniper, beech, and flowering quince.

Neagari
Nay-AY-gah-ree

RAISED ROOT

This extraordinary style, in which a tree trunk floats in the air on woody stilt-like roots, originates in extreme natural events. In one scenario, a tree growing by a river has the soil beneath it washed away in a flood; in another, an isolated tree growing on a precipice survives when the rocky soil on which it grows disappears in a landslide. Sometimes growers train the exposed roots close together. As the roots thicken, they fuse into a solid gnarly mass akin to a trunk. Trees in the raised-root style have a timeworn primeval

Raised-root bonsai have bowed trunks and woody roots poised above the soil.

look that increases as the exposed roots thicken. Interpreted by bonsai artists, the tree should look bent and ravaged by the elements but also be pervaded by a sense of inner balance and serenity. One way to train a raised-root bonsai is to set the plant in a deep container filled with crumbly potting mix, then trim the ends of the principal roots to encourage fine threadlike roots to develop at the tips. The raised-root style is appropriate for many plants, including black pine, white pine, serissa, and numerous succulents.

Bankan
BAHN-kahn

COILED TRUNK

While gentle S-curves characterize the tree in the informal-upright style, the coiled style has a twisted trunk with spiraling bends resembling coiled snakes. In nature, coiled trees grow on plains and mountains. Their gnarled trunks emulate the effects of advanced age. When the trunk rises straight from the base, the roots

Bonsai trees with coiled trunks exhibit dramatic movement and gnarly beauty in their design.

radiate in all directions to give visual support and stability to the tree's bent but elegant shape. When a tree rises angled from its base, more roots should be visible inside the angle in order to balance the weight of the tipped trunk. Ideally, the branches form a rounded triangle that brings order to the dramatic form of the trunk. The treetop tips slightly forward, its leafy canopy leaving the fluid lines of the trunk exposed. Both evergreen and deciduous trees make excellent coiled-trunk bonsai.

ROCK GROWING

Rock-grown bonsai symbolizes the harshness of nature. It embodies trees growing on rock face, the soil eroded by wind, rain, or snow. You can find these trees growing in rocky clefts, suspended from cliffs, or clasping a crag or a boulder in a lake. Some of these trees survive in mountain soil pockets. Others exist with the top of their roots gripping rock and the bottom planted in the earth from which the rock emerges (*sekijojuku* style). Bonsai makers collect jagged or irregular rocks for

this form of bonsai, creating mountains in a dish. Since this style of bonsai is by nature insecure, the grower has to attach the tree to the rock by artificial means such as wire and glue. Most trees are suitable for rock growing, as long as they are shaped to grow in harmony with the rock that supports them.

A trident maple forms strong woody roots that cling to the rock on the way to the nourishing soil.

GROUP PLANTING

Group plantings can represent trees in a conifer forest, an orchard, or deciduous woods—any situation where a large number of trees grow together in the landscape. Whereas a multitrunk bonsai grows from one set of roots, group plantings combine individual trees, each grown on its own roots. Thus a multitrunk bonsai will have more unity because the size, color, and texture of its leaves will be the same. The foliage of a group planting, however, may vary even when the trees belong to the same species. When planning a group planting,

use an odd number of trees up to 15. After that, it doesn't matter, since people will see masses and not individual trunks. No matter how many trees are in a group planting, the trunks should not overlap from any viewpoint. Vary the space between trees and their age, height, and diameter. Then situate the trees however you like. Divide them into groups by size or shape (straight, curved, or windswept), or set them on mounds of soil that simulate undulating foothills.

'Catlin' lacebark elms grow on a rock slab to simulate landscape conditions.

TRAY LANDSCAPE

In bonsai, a single tree embodies the mood of an entire landscape. In saikei, the picturesque landscape prevails. These living miniature landscapes depict scenes of mountains, hills, and water by combining rocks, diminutive trees, grasses, gravel, moss, and tiny alpine flowers in the correct scale and proportions. Tray landscapes can be short-term projects that are easy and inexpensive to make. They often use more than one type of tree, unlike bonsai,, where one tree species is

the norm. Saikei trees tend to be younger than bonsai and may be removed from the saikei tray and potted up as individual bonsai as they mature. Rocks are partly buried, then covered with moss to resemble a mountaintop or the outcropping of a ledge.

Tray landscapes re-create vast natural scenes on a minute scale with tiny rocks and plants.

Displaying Your Bonsai

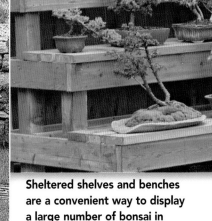

Sheltered shelves and benches are a convenient way to display a large number of bonsai in limited outdoor space.

Stone or concrete pillars hold these bonsai near eye level, keeping them undamaged and off the ground.

Indoors, a bonsai looks best silhouetted against a neutral wall for contrast.

Showing off your bonsai is as much an art as growing it. To best appreciate a bonsai tree, you need to see it at eye level with the center of the trunk at the same height as your eyes. Silhouetting bonsai against a plain wall on an uncluttered table or stand focuses the attention on the plant. Following some basic guidelines will help you create the perfect presentation both indoors and outdoors.

Outdoor displays

Display hardy bonsai trees outdoors. Conifers such as pine, spruce, and hemlock and deciduous trees such as maples, elms, and beeches need a period of winter dormancy. Because their roots are more vulnerable to damage than those of trees planted in the ground, they also need shelter from harsh winds, glaring afternoon sun, and extreme temperatures. Find a growing spot that is pleasant and sunny, protected from wind, and large enough for you to perform routine plant maintenance. Make sure your display area is near the house to maximize your enjoyment of the trees.

Since bonsai trees are short, exhibit them on stands, tables, walls, shelves, or pedestals that make them easier to see. If you install a display shelf against the bare wall of a garage, for example, make sure that air can circulate around the plants and that heat radiating from the wall does not bake your bonsai. Rotate trees from time to time to keep the growth from becoming lopsided, and water them regularly. Around the perimeter of a small lawn or courtyard, you can build wooden benches or open shelves set on concrete blocks. If you grow many bonsai trees, step the shelves down like bleachers to take full advantage of the space. Place shelves and benches high enough to keep cascading plants from touching the ground.

To focus attention on a special tree, place it on a simple pedestal or column of wood, brick, or concrete topped with a stable platform. Pedestals provide excellent viewing from all sides, and you can cluster them at different heights to display a group of trees. Avoid setting the columns in straight lines, and leave enough room between them to ensure good viewing, proper maintenance, and air circulation. Exhibit a big bonsai alone and assemble small trees in a pleasing group.

Bonsai trees on stands also make attractive decorations for wooden decks and stone patios. To help you determine the height of the display, decide whether you will be sitting or standing when you look at your bonsai.

Inside views

In American homes where patterned wallpaper and knickknack-covered tables are the norm, finding the right place for bonsai can be a challenge. The larger the bonsai, the more space you need to appreciate it. Traditionally, the Japanese display bonsai against a white background in a vestiblue or alcove in the most important room in the home. The tree sits on a wooden table, shelf, or pedestal that complements

its shape. Nearby is an interesting rock or a small pot of ornamental grass, and on the wall hangs a scroll with painting or calligraphy. The accessories heighten awareness of the bonsai. Without distractions the tree becomes the central focus, filling the minds of those who see it with appreciation for its natural form.

To adapt these ideas to your own house, put your bonsai on a wooden or bamboo stand. You can also set it on a bamboo mat, a stone slab, or a flat chunk of wood. Make the stand bigger than the pot so that it sets the bonsai apart from the table.

Simplify the background by placing the bonsai against a blank wall or bamboo screen.

Although tropical and subtropical plants work best for year-round indoor bonsai display, from time to time you may want to bring a hardy bonsai into the house. You can bring one inside for a few days at a time but no longer. Keep it watered and away from radiators, fireplaces, and drafty doors and windows. By following these guidelines, you can show the fragrant blooms of the crabapple, the fruits of flowering quince, and the red and yellow fall leaves of the Japanese maple and the maidenhair tree.

Because of its tiny size, *mame* bonsai looks best displayed in groups on special bonsai stands.

A fine decorative shelf displays *mame* trees and pots to advantage.

A cascade bonsai sits near a table's edge so the crown can grow downward below the pot.

Getting Started

If bonsai piques your imagination but you don't know where to begin, then reading this chapter is the next step on your journey to growing miniature trees. You will learn how to recognize a good bonsai plant at a nursery and how to buy a mail-order plant. You will also discover easy ways to propagate a plant of your own.

Visit a bonsai nursery to see miniature trees at various stages of bonsai training.

Buying plants for bonsai

AT A GARDEN CENTER: If you understand the plant characteristics necessary for creating bonsai, you may find good material at a reputable nursery or garden center near your home. Look for one-gallon containers holding healthy trees with vigorous root systems radiating around the trunk. Roots can be narrow or thick but should not encircle the base of the tree since girdling roots can kill it. Ideally, the trunk is rounded and unscarred. It should flare at the base and taper as it rises, but pruning techniques may also thicken the trunk and shape the tree.

For quick shaping results, look for a branch one-third of the way up the trunk to use as a bottom branch on one side of the tree. It should be one-third or less of the trunk's diameter where they join. See if there is a second branch on the opposite side but higher on the trunk; then look for a branch in back above or between the other two. The side branches should come slightly forward.

The tree you choose should look strong with no signs of damage. Rough broken twigs and branches indicate that the plant has been damaged in shipping or in handling at the garden center. If the plant is in leaf, choose foliage that looks healthy and is the right color for the season and the variety. Do not buy plants with wilted leaves or brown leaf margins, which are signs of inappropriate watering. Brown or black leaf spots, streaky leaves or black areas on the stem point to disease.

AT A BONSAI NURSERY: When you visit a nursery or shop specializing in trained bonsai, you will find plants in various stages of bonsai training. Keep in mind what location you have set aside for your bonsai, whether you want a temperate or tropical plant, and any special look or effect you may want. Trees should sit firmly in their containers and be well-rooted in the soil. Trunks should have an attractive broad base and taper toward the top to give the bonsai a feeling of stability. The bottom branch should start about one-third of the way up the trunk with branches gradually tapering

from base to tip. These branches should be few but well-placed and effective.

Nurseries use many methods to propagate pre-bonsai. Some are made from cuttings of desirable plants, while others grow from the tissue of a sought-after plant grafted onto another plant's vigorous root stock. Cutting-propagated bonsai grow more slowly than grafted plants. They have no graft rings and may display less tapered trunks with no graft rings. On the other hand, a poorly grafted tree may be hard to train and maintain. If you select a grafted tree, make sure that the graft union is low and the bark of both trees matches above and below the graft site. If the graft is too high, the tree can develop a reverse taper.

Choose a plant with a balanced, graceful, natural shape without any awkward distortions. The soil surface should feel dense and solid and be completely covered with gravel, moss, or a combination of both. A superior old bonsai costs more than a young one being trained. Pricing is also based on the plant's rarity, the quality of a mature bonsai's training, and the tree's overall condition and character.

MAIL-ORDER BONSAI:
Although you cannot see what you are buying when you purchase trees on the Internet or from a catalog, you have at your fingertips an endless array of specialized stock. This book contains Resources pages with names of some reputable mail-order nurseries. These are good places to begin your mail-order search. Mail-order trees are typically rooted cuttings, seedlings, divisions, or grafts. The catalog may state how plants are propagated, or you can phone the nursery for that information. Shipping policies differ for each nursery, but plants shipped during dormancy from November to April may be shipped bare root or semibare root. Follow the planting directions that come with each tree as soon as it arrives.

CHECKING FOR THE GRAFT UNION

Recognizing a successful bonsai graft is important when buying a nursery-grown tree. Here's a to-do list when shopping for bonsai stock:
■ Look for a graft mark as near the roots as possible. Root grafts performed on stem tissue below the crown where the root stem and the true stem meet are best, since the graft bump will be at soil level and look like the swelling of the roots.
■ Avoid trees where the graft union is high on the trunk. As the plant ages, this area may become swollen, unsightly, and develop an undesirable reverse taper.
■ Make sure the bark above the graft is similar to the bark below it. Otherwise, the trunk will look ugly and unnatural.
■ Watch out for suckers, vigorous shoots sprouting from the root stock, because heavy suckering means heavy pruning. For instance, the root stock used with varieties of cherry, apricot, and plum trees (*Prunus* spp.) can be so strong that it sends up constant shoots that have to be removed. If you let the tree sucker, you will ruin the balanced look of the bonsai. Furthermore, rampant suckers can destroy your bonsai by drawing energy away from the grafted scion (shoot portion of the graft).
■ If the plants constituting the graft grow at drastically different rates, distortions in the trunk may result. A fast-growing scion will make the trunk fatter above the graft union than below, while fast-growing understock will do the opposite.

Starting Your Own Bonsai

For good germination, vary the planting depth and starting time according to the seed you grow.

After the first set of true leaves emerge or if leaves look yellow, feed seedlings with granular or half-strength liquid fertilizer.

Starting your own seed

If you want to grow bonsai from trees in the wild, starting your bonsai from seed is the most economical and ecologically sound way to do it. This method requires patience, because the tree won't be ready to train for a year or two and the bonsai form may not appear for another five years. For discerning growers, however, it is worth the wait to control the shaping from the start and to create a perfect tree. *Mame* bonsai, which stand about 6 inches tall, work well when started from seed.

■ **Collect ripe seeds in the fall.** Seeds vary in size. Colorful crabapple fruit *(Malus)* and holly berries *(Ilex)* contain seeds, as do

acorns, beechnuts, and the propellers that float to the ground from maple trees *(Acer)*. You can also buy bonsai seeds for popular tree species. Follow directions on the seed packet for germination procedures.

■ **Seed-starting times are based on where you live and the seed varieties you are planting.** Some seeds need to break dormancy before they will germinate. Depending on the type of seed, you may have to refrigerate it in moist sand for several weeks or months. Other seeds require their hard coats to be broken by cracking, sanding, or nicking before germination. For tips on starting specific seeds in your area, contact your local cooperative extension office.

Remove a leaf from a jade plant with a clean knife or use a fallen leaf to start a new plant. Let the leaf sit for a couple of days until a callus forms at the leaf base.

Rooting in water

■ **English ivy** *(Hedera helix)* makes an interesting bonsai subject. You can propagate it by removing a stem tip and placing it in tap water until it roots. Other bonsai plants such as willow *(Salix)*, coleus *(Solenostemon scutellarioides)*, and Japanese gray-bark elm *(Zelkova)* may also be rooted this way.

Leaf-bud cuttings

■ **Jade plant** *(Crassula ovata)* is easy to propagate from cut or fallen leaves or stems. When a leaf drops off your plant, let it stay where it lands for a day or two; then insert the hardened leaf base into fast-draining potting mix. The leaf must also contain a bud or piece from the stem, or the cutting will develop

roots but no new stem. Similarly, you can root a stem by letting a callous form over the break or cut and then inserting the base of the stem into a small container filled with fast-draining potting mix. Rooting occurs in about two weeks. Wait until the new plant is established before feeding it with fertilizer and training it as a bonsai tree.

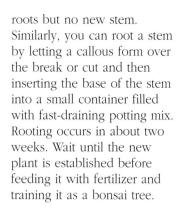

Poke a hole in the potting mix with a pencil tip and stick the leaf in the hole, leaving the rounded top exposed.

Stem cuttings

■ **You can propagate most plants from cuttings, a quicker way than starting from seed.** Unlike some seedlings, plants made from cuttings look exactly like their parent. The process is simple. With a sterile knife or pruner, remove a 4-inch piece from the tip of a healthy branch or stem. Strip the leaves on the bottom half of the stem, take off any flower buds, apply rooting hormone, and stick the lower one-third of the stem into growing medium. Insert the cutting at the desired angle to create sloping, coiled, or windswept styles. Keep moist. Start cuttings in late spring before the buds open and in early summer after new growth has hardened. Exact timing depends upon the type of plant you want to propagate.

With sterile scissors, nip the tip of a healthy twig or branch.

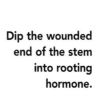

Dip the wounded end of the stem into rooting hormone.

Set the cuttings into a tray of fast-draining rooting medium. To aid the rooting process, warm the medium by placing the tray on a heating mat.

Layering

■ **Layering is frequently seen in nature.** This layering on forsythia, dogwood, viburnum, and rhododendron occurs when a low or bent branch touches the earth and takes root while attached to the parent plant. You can cut the new plant free from the parent, dig it, and move it to a new location. Likewise, you can create a layered plant from a low, well-shaped flexible branch. Lower the branch to the ground, marking a spot about 12 inches from the branch tip. Dig a trench 4 inches deep at the site. Mix compost into the soil dug from the hole. Remove leaves from the stem and make a shallow cut on the bottom of the branch where it will sit in the ground. Keep the cut open by placing a stone in it. Set the branch in the hole, pegging it to keep the cut in the ground and, if necessary, staking the branch tip to keep it upright. Within a few months, the new plant should be ready to harvest.

Step one: First, cut a 4-inch-deep channel about 1 foot from the branch tip.

Step two: Notch the branch bottom, then peg it into the ground

Step three: After several months sever the rooted branch tip with a sharp spade or shovel.

Potting & Repotting

This chapter deals with potting up plants that you have bought or propagated. Most healthy potted plants need repotting at some stage of their growth, but that process occurs with regularity for bonsai trees growing in shallow containers. Bonsai live for many years, so repotting and soils are very important. Potting soil must be fast draining yet able to retain some moisture because most bonsai need daily watering. Along with the basics for repotting trees in a safe and timely way, you will also discover guidelines for choosing the right container for your particular plant.

The Repotting Advantage

REPOTTING IMPROVES SOIL TEXTURE: Soil in a pot breaks down over time. Passing seasons, daily maintenance, and the increasing pressure of thick, aging roots make soil less porous.

REPOTTING BRINGS VITAL OXYGEN TO THE ROOTS: The increasingly fine texture of old soil keeps adequate oxygen from reaching the roots of plants. Fresh, porous soil allows oxygen to circulate to the roots during watering.

REPOTTING AIDS NUTRIENT ASSIMILATION: When a bonsai is pot-bound, there is no room for new root growth. New roots assimilate nutrients efficiently. The repotting process includes cutting away old roots to make space for new ones.

REPOTTING HELPS WATER RETENTION: The water-holding characteristics of bonsai soil break down with time. Fresh, porous soil holds water long enough for plant roots to absorb it.

REPOTTING REDUCES PESTS AND DISEASES: When you remove a plant from its pot and discard the old soil, you can inspect the roots for potential problems. If you see signs of insects or diseases, you can deal with them before they harm the plant.

REPOTTING KEEPS YOUR BONSAI SMALL: Changing the soil goes hand in hand with root pruning, which makes it possible for your plant to return to the same container. Repotting is one of several elements in the dwarfing process that keeps your bonsai small and healthy.

REPOTTING CAN CHANGE THE LOOK OF YOUR BONSAI: When you repot, you can replace the plant in its original container or find a dish in a different shape or color to enhance your bonsai. The relationship between plant and pot is crucial to successful bonsai design.

Potting up

For the first year or two of making a bonsai, keep the plant in its original pot and leave the roots alone. Start shaping the top of the plant by pruning up to one-third of the foliage at a time, making sure you give the plant several months to recover before pruning it again. When the tree is ready to transplant, choose a bonsai training pot, which is a big version of a bonsai dish. Your bonsai will spend its early years in this container. A training pot has large drainage holes and is big enough to contain the young tree's system of thick and thin roots. Over the next few years, when you repot the tree in training you will cut back about one-third to one-half of its roots, including the taproot, to promote a network of fine fibrous roots.

Repotting schedule

The time to repot bonsai depends on the plant you are growing. Sometimes pot-bound roots can grow through the drainage holes on the bottom or push the plant upward in its container. You can also check the root system by gently lifting the tree from its container. It is time to repot when you see elongated roots circling a solid root mass that extends to the edge of the dish. Many deciduous trees need repotting every two years, although young apricot, cherry, and plum trees (*Prunus* spp.) are repotted each year. Conifers require repotting every two to five years, depending upon the tree's age and species. The best season to repot most hardy trees is spring, before budding begins.

Potting turntable

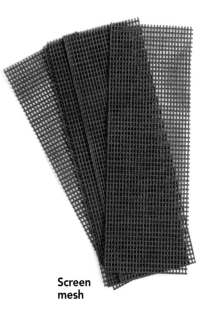

Screen mesh

Potting necessities

SCREEN/MESH: These are used to cover the drainage holes of a bonsai dish. Bonsai growers screen dust particles from their potting mix to ensure quick drainage. A $\frac{1}{16}$-inch screen or a window screen works well to remove the dust.

POTTING SOIL: Different trees benefit from different types of soil because they have varying abilities to hold water and nutrients. Some growers place soils with different particle sizes at different levels in the container. Consider the following:

■ **Soilless growing medium:** Mix equal parts of perlite and peat moss to make your own soilless growing medium.

■ **Specialized potting mixes:** Rhododendron and azalea (*Rhododendron* spp.), holly (*Ilex* spp.), enkianthus, and other ericaceous plants thrive in acid soil with a higher proportion of peat. Tropical and subtropical plants prefer a slower draining potting mix than most bonsai.

■ **Homemade potting mix:** Use equal parts organic (pine bark, fir bark, or peat), mineral (sharp sand, volcanic gravel, or hyalite), and clay.

GROUNDCOVER: This will give your bonsai a finished look. Use any of the following groundcovers:

■ **Baby tears,** *Soleirolia soleirolii,* has yellowish green, round leaves and white flowers. It needs frequent watering and careful handling.

■ **Corsican mint,** *Mentha requienii,* has scented leaves. It is good for Zone 7, grows to 1 inch high, and should be kept moist.

■ **Elfin thyme,** *Thymus serpyllum* 'Minus', is an evergreen with pink flowers. It is good for Zone 5 and conserves water, growing about 1–2 inches high.

■ **Fujiyama bonsai moss** is a fine moss.

■ **Iron stones** 2-4 millimeters in diameter are especially good for indoors.

Homemade potting mix

Moss

■ **Lichen** is a combination of moss and algae.

■ **Pebbles, sand, or small gravel** make effective earth-tone groundcovers.

■ **Scotch moss** is a dark evergreen. Mosses should cover no more than one-third of the soil because they can absorb water and nutrients intended for the tree. Remove moss from outdoor trees to use on your bonsai soil.

Try gravel in earthy hues to cover exposed bonsai soil. Avoid limestone which can raise pH.

Potting mix

The Repotting Advantage
(continued)

Potting tools and accessories

■ **SIEVE:** holder with screen sets in different sizes for sifting fine particles from the soil

■ **BROOM:** brushes soil smooth on the surface

■ **GARDEN TOOL SET:** usually holds a mini rake, trowel, hoe, and weeding tools

■ **SHEARS/SCISSORS:** cuts off old roots

■ **ROOT HOOK OR PICK:** combs out roots before pruning

■ **SOIL SCOOP:** comes in different sizes for moving potting soil into the potting dish

■ **SOIL CHOPSTICKS:** take off old soil from bonsai; push fresh soil around newly pruned roots during potting

■ **DIRT PATTER:** tamps moss around the bonsai

■ **PLASTIC DRAINAGE MESH:** sits over drainage holes in pot

■ **TRANSPLANTING SPATULA:** works along the edge of the dish to free the root mass

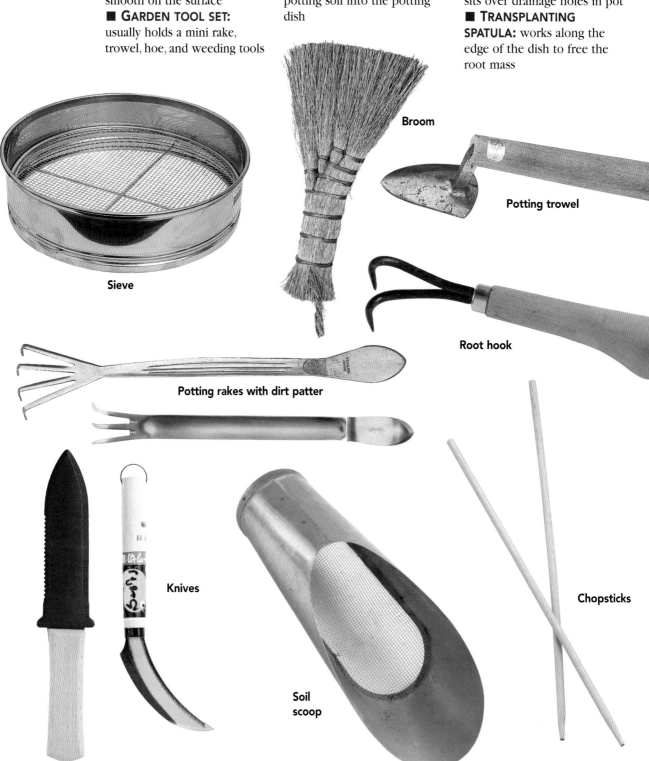

Broom

Potting trowel

Sieve

Root hook

Potting rakes with dirt patter

Knives

Soil scoop

Chopsticks

Repotting Step-by-Step

1. Making certain the soil is slightly dry, loosen the edge of the bonsai with a transplanting spatula and then lift the plant carefully by the trunk. When bonsai roots look congested and circle around themselves at the edge of the root mass, it is time to repot.

2. Holding the tree trunk, take off about half of the old soil with a chopstick.

3. Use a root pick to comb out roots before pruning.

Repotting Step-by-Step
(continued)

4. With shears, prune roots that are damaged, rotten, thick, or very long. Cut back the bottom of the root mass by one-third.

5. Cover drainage holes of container with plastic mesh and secure with copper or anodized aluminum wire. Drainage pebbles may also be used at the bottom of the pot.

6. Once you determine a harmonious location for the tree inside the pot, set the root ball in place and wire it into the dish to hold it in place. The root crown can be a bit higher than the edge of the pot.

7. Scoop soil into the container with the soil scoop; using chopsticks, pack soil around the roots.

8. Tamp the soil with the dirt patter, particularly around the edge of the dish below the rim.

9. Screen a thin layer of soil on top of the potting soil. Tamp the soil again.

Repotting Step-by-Step
(continued)

10. Use the broom to smooth the soil surface, which should be just below the pot rim.

11. Water the bonsai thoroughly.

12. Add moss, decorative gravel, or another groundcover to the soil surface. Pat again. Keep the repotted bonsai in a shaded area sheltered from winds until new growth appears. After the initial thorough watering, water less frequently than usual and avoid fertilizing until new growth appears.

Containers: Joining tradition with personal taste

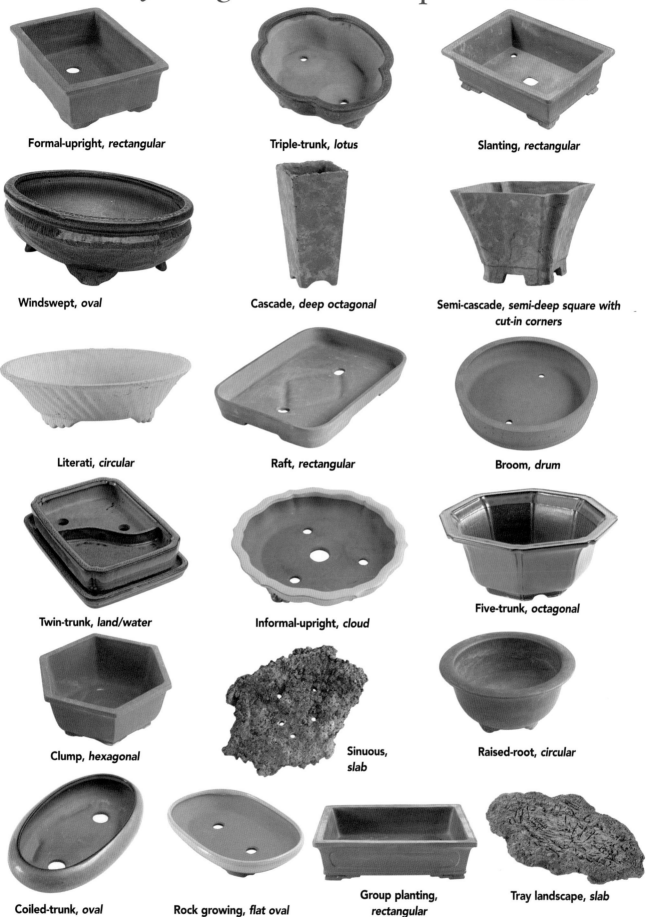

Formal-upright, *rectangular*

Triple-trunk, *lotus*

Slanting, *rectangular*

Windswept, *oval*

Cascade, *deep octagonal*

Semi-cascade, *semi-deep square with cut-in corners*

Literati, *circular*

Raft, *rectangular*

Broom, *drum*

Twin-trunk, *land/water*

Informal-upright, *cloud*

Five-trunk, *octagonal*

Clump, *hexagonal*

Sinuous, *slab*

Raised-root, *circular*

Coiled-trunk, *oval*

Rock growing, *flat oval*

Group planting, *rectangular*

Tray landscape, *slab*

Containers
(continued)

Most pots come in muted hues. Shapes, textures, and finishes vary from plain to picturesque.

Personalize your bonsai by choosing handmade or freestyle pots.

In the art of bonsai, the container is an integral part of the final design. A bonsai dish must meet the physical requirements of your tree in terms of size, depth, and drainage. Its shape, color, material, and finish should also harmonize with the tree's style and features such as bark, fruit, flowers, and foliage. Choose a pot that pleases you and enhances the appearance of your bonsai. When it is time to repot your tree, you can reuse the same container or find another more to your liking.

Bonsai pots share certain physical characteristics, including feet to raise the dish and promote drainage and air circulation. Containers need drainage holes 10 millimeters or .4 inches wide. When repotting a mature specimen, avoid containers with grooved or dimpled interiors since water can gather in low spots and rot the roots.

You can find a vast selection of bonsai containers at specialized nurseries, Oriental shops, and on the Internet. Elegant Japanese ceramics; decorative Chinese porcelain; plastic pots; and slabs of slate, granite, and fiberglass are available, ranging in price from a few to thousands of dollars. Tokoname ceramic pots from Japan are among the finest in quality and style. Consider starting out with an inexpensive training pot and graduating to better-quality pots as you grow in expertise.

While there are no absolute rules to choosing bonsai dishes, the following elements may guide your choice:

Tree placement

■ Do not center a bonsai tree in its pot. If you were to divide your container into quadrants, you would set the tree in a rear quadrant in back of an imaginary midline. The exact spot depends upon the slant, style, and thickness of the bonsai tree.
■ Trees in straight or curved upright styles should be planted at one-third the length of oval or rectangular containers.
■ A right-leaning tree would sit left of center in its container; a left-leaning tree would be on the right.
■ When branching is denser on the right side of the tree, the tree should sit on the left and vice-versa.
■ A tree positioned too far front, back, or to the side upsets the stability of the composition.
■ A cascade or semi-cascade bonsai that drops to the left needs elongated roots on the opposite side from the slant for balance. To secure the plant in the pot, these long roots would be planted to the right of center in the pot.

Pot shape

■ Cascades and semi-cascades need deeper pots to balance the downward sweep of the branches. These vertical pots recall the natural bluffs where you would find a cascading plant.

To maintain visual equilibrium, a left-leaning pine is anchored on the right side of its container.

The right dish complements the size and style of the plant.

■ In containers with asymmetrical rims, the lower part should face front.

■ The height of the dish and the diameter of the trunk should be the same.

■ A deep, substantial dish balances a tree with a heavy trunk and thick canopy of leaves.

■ The width of a pot should be two-thirds the width of a broad tree's canopy or two-thirds the height of a tall tree.

■ Small round dishes suit literati-style trees.

■ Group plantings go well with slabs of rock or fiberglass and in wide flat containers.

■ The scale of the dish must suit the tree.

Pot colors

■ Brown unglazed pots are acceptable with most trees.

■ Conifers look best in brown or dark-colored unglazed dishes.

■ *Mame* bonsai look good in more colorful pots. Bright colors have more impact than neutral tones and help balance the trees with their tiny containers.

■ Avoid containers that are glazed inside since glazing can affect drainage and ultimately cause root rot. Glazed interiors may also keep the roots from adhering to container sides, thus making the plant unstable in the pot when moved.

■ Trees with colorful deciduous or evergreen leaves look good in glazed or unglazed, colorful pots. Green goes with most leaf colors.

■ Trees with fruit also suit colorful pots: try white pots with red-fruited trees and blue pots for trees with yellow or orange fruit.

The width of a bonsai dish should be two-thirds the height of the tree it contains.

A medium-deep pot balances the descending curve of this California live oak bonsai in the semi-cascade style. *Right,* A jade plant is too small for its dish.

Pruning & Shaping

A bristlecone pine shows the dead naked branches that bonsai artists describe as *jin*.

Pruning and shaping a bonsai affect the size, contour, and scale of its parts. Timely pruning assists the dwarfing process, and shaping transforms your small tree into a bonsai. This chapter will show you some pruning and shaping techniques in a simple step-by-step format. You will also learn which tools make these techniques easier and how you use various tools.

Remember, when you prune a bonsai, you make real your mental image of a tree's ideal form. This perfect shape displays all the characteristics of the tree in its natural habitat. The environment where the tree grows shapes it. If an elm grows in the midst of a sunny field with ample water and nourishment, it will be upright with full leafy branches and a thick, handsome trunk. If the conditions are windy, over time the tree branches will bend where they are blown. If a pine grows on a cliff, erosion can pull it over the edge. The forces of nature balance each other to keep the tree alive. Your job is to study the plant you are shaping, understand its place in nature, and visualize what it can become. Thus the ultimate form of your bonsai will vary by the nature of the plant you choose, the style or natural situation that you want to mimic, and your vision and technical skills.

Pruning Tools

CONCAVE BRANCH CUTTER: Unfamiliar to gardeners in the Western hemisphere, this tool cuts branches back from

bonsai trunks and main branches without leaving a noticeable mark. Because these angled cutters scoop some tissue from the trunk or main stem where the lesser branch was attached, they leave a dent in the surface. When a scar forms, raising the level of the indentation, it heals level with the surrounding plane. Regular pruners, on the other hand, leave either a bump of raised scar tissue or a stub at the base of a pruned branch. Variations of concave branch cutters include curved jaws, narrow blades, and different handle lengths.

UTILITY/LARGE-HANDLE BONSAI SHEARS: These large, heavy-duty 8-inch scissors have big bowed handles and sharp, short (2- to 3-inch) blades. Beginner-grade shears have short, thick blades while the blades of professional-grade shears are longer and narrower. You can prune small bonsai branches and remove leaves with them, as well as use them for a number of outdoor garden pruning jobs.

TRIMMING SHEARS/BONSAI SCISSORS: Standard 8-inch scissors have long, straight handles for control over fine tasks. The narrow 2½-inch blades and straight handles allow you to trim in tight spots. They work well for interior leaf and branch pruning and for creating *mame* bonsai.

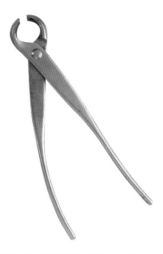

BUD AND DETAIL SHEARS:
Bonsai growers use this
scissor for detail work.
It is the tool of choice
for trimming pine candles
(partially expanded shoots) in
the spring. You can also use it
for taking off faded azalea
blossoms and the detailed
pruning of *mame* bonsai.

CHOPSTICKS: Chopsticks take
off old soil from bonsai and
push fresh soil around newly
pruned roots during potting.

KNOB CUTTER: This tool
eliminates knobs and stubs
from trunks and branches.
It also takes round chunks
of wood off a surface that
has been pruned or sawed
flat. Making the flat wound
concave ensures that the
pruned trunk or branch
will heal level with the
surrounding surface.

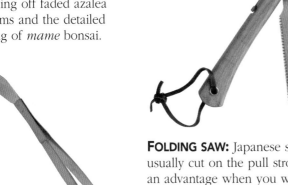

FOLDING SAW: Japanese saws
usually cut on the pull stroke,
an advantage when you want
a neat, even slice. You can
use a folding saw to sever big
branches and trunks when
pruning or shaping.

CUT PASTE: This mixture seals
large pruning cuts and helps
heal wounds to a tree.
It keeps the cut from drying
out and shields it from
invasive pests and diseases
that could enter the tree
through an open wound.
Cut paste comes in tubes
or jars. Apply it with your
fingers, smoothing it over the
wound and beyond the edges
to seal it. As the tree grows
and the wound heals, new
wood forms over the spot.

TWEEZERS: Tweezers are
useful for taking buds and
needles off pine trees without
harming other needle bundles,
buds, or branches. Tweezers'
tips vary. Some are straight,
some bent, some serrated to
improve their grip. The choice
is up to you. Manufacturers
also supply tools that have
tweezers at one end and a
miniature garden implement
such as a trowel or spatula
at the other.

ROOT HOOK, PICK, OR RAKE:
This hook is a rake with one
or two tines that can reach
inside a root ball to separate
or comb out entangled roots
before pruning.

Pruning Step-by-Step

Brilliant fall color enhances the elegant form of most Japanese maples.

tree. But most plants adapted as bonsai respond well to severe pruning, so damage is unlikely. Even if you lose a plant, you can learn from a mistake. It is in the nature of plants to grow, and many missteps are correctable with time. Respect the flow of the plant. Keep in mind the image you seek to create, removing both crossed branches and jutting frontal branches. Don't expect instant mastery. Bonsai growers practice these techniques for years, developing new twists on old methods. Given a little time, you can polish your skills and create an approach to bonsai that's uniquely your own.

Tip dominance: room at the top

I n the previous chapter, you learned how to prune a tree below the soil surface. This chapter will show you several basic techniques for pruning the top of a plant. In the beginning, they may look drastic, and you may feel as if you are destroying or disfiguring your

Trees grow faster at the tip, or apex, than they do at the bottom. The term for this phenomenon is apical dominance. The same growth hormone that makes trees more vigorous at the top than

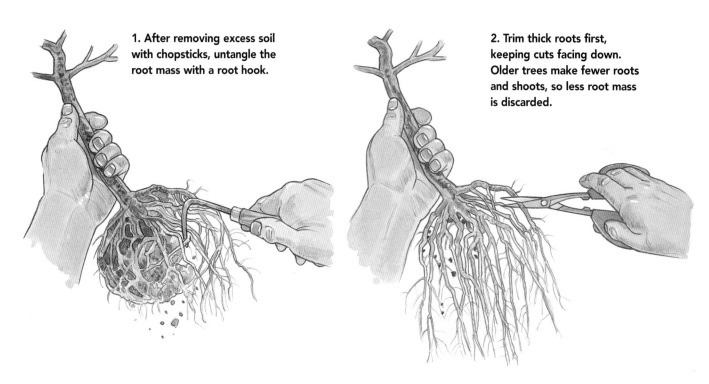

1. After removing excess soil with chopsticks, untangle the root mass with a root hook.

2. Trim thick roots first, keeping cuts facing down. Older trees make fewer roots and shoots, so less root mass is discarded.

in the lower parts of the plant causes a branch to lengthen at the tip rather than at the base. In bonsai, timely pruning checks the fast growth of the treetop and invigorates the slow-growing lower branches, thus maintaining the unity of the tree's canopy and preserving its style. To shape your bonsai, prune old wood after the tree has gone dormant in late fall. Prune new growth during the growing season to maintain the bonsai's shape. Cutting off the growing tips of upper branches promotes more vigorous growth in the lower branches. Therefore, if you remove the two end nodes (places on a branch where buds or branches form) of a three-node branch, you disrupt apical dominance. You can shorten the branch, thus encouraging buds to open behind the pinched off tips. Instead of a long shoot with long spaces between leaves or buds, buds will open lower on the stem,

which can split into two shorter stems with smaller spaces between leaves. The happy result for your bonsai is a dwarfed, twiggy branch.

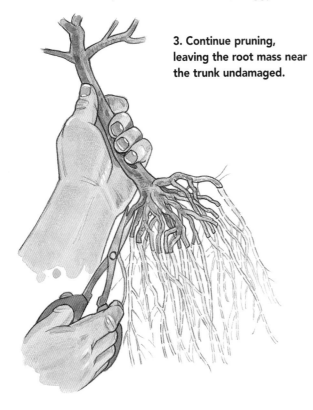

3. Continue pruning, leaving the root mass near the trunk undamaged.

Root pruning

Root pruning occurs during the repotting process (see pages 29–30). It decreases the root mass by at least one-third and can place significant stress on a bonsai tree. By keeping the inner root mass closest to the trunk unharmed when pruning, your bonsai will remain strong and healthy. Necessary tools for pruning include a root hook and shears. Shears should be clean and sharp before cutting to avoid spreading disease from plant to plant. You may notice that old trees produce fewer roots than young ones, so there is less to prune. Root pruning decreases the volume of woody old roots in the pot and increases the number of fine moist roots. When you remove the ends of old roots, make sure your cuts are clean and sharp to promote young fibrous roots.

A tree grows fastest at the top and the upper branch tips because of apical dominance.

Pruning Step-by-Step
(continued)

Candling pines

Candles are the growth shoots of pines *(Pinus)*. To control and refine the lines of this bonsai, break off the candles with your fingers—a process known as candling. Scissoring candles can damage needle tips and turn them brown.

Candling forces the whorled buds at the base of the shoot to grow. The second growth is less vigorous than the first although the candle's ultimate size depends on when you candle it. To break a candle, hold the branch in one hand. In your other hand, take the shoot between the thumb and forefinger. Pull the shoot toward you. It should break off at its base. You can remove partial candles as well as the whole candle, depending on the growth you want to stimulate. Check the plant selection guide in Chapter 8 to determine the best time to prune for your particular pine species.

1. Pines form candles at the tips of growing shoots.

Finger pruning conifers

Similarly, trim conifers with scalelike foliage such as juniper *(Juniperus)* and false cypress *(Chamaecyparis)* by taking the end of the branch being pruned in one hand and the shoot you are removing in the other. Instead of plucking the tip shoot straight out, twist the shoot and tug until it breaks off.

2. Candle pines in late spring when shoots are soft and needles on the candle are still short. The more of the candle you remove, the more you restrict tree growth.

Leaf pruning needled conifers

Study an old needled conifer in nature: Foliage grows on the branch top but not the bottom. Moreover, the foliage on old trees grows toward the branch tip, where it receives maximum light. To increase the appearance of age in a needled bonsai, pluck needles from the undersides of branches. In order to see the branch and trunk structure, remove leaves and twigs from the joint between the trunk and the branch. Hold the branch in one hand and carefully pluck needle bundles with the thumb and forefinger of your other hand.

Reduce needle size and thin foliage on 2-needled pines by removing all needles below the top five or six pairs. Prune in fall with long, fine-bladed scissors.

Cut leaves off deciduous trees at their base, keeping leaf stalks on the tree. The stalks will drop off later. Leaf pruning decreases leaf size and promotes more intense fall color.

Leaf pruning

Defoliating, or leaf pruning, entails removing from two-thirds to all of the leaves of a deciduous bonsai in early summer. Working from top to bottom, cut leaves off at their base with sharp scissors, leaving the petioles (leaf stalks), which fall off later. Leaf trimming reduces the leaf size of wide-leaf deciduous bonsai such as maple *(Acer)* and elm *(Ulmus)* so that the leaves are in natural proportion to the dwarfed tree. A defoliated tree thinks it has lived through winter, thus inducing two seasons of growth in one. Leaf pruning also intensifies fall leaf color. Because defoliation is stressful on the tree, keep your bonsai vigorous and watered well before you attempt this procedure. Do not defoliate and repot a bonsai in the same year, and never defoliate a tree that exhibits nonvigorous growth.

Pruning Step-by-Step
(continued)

During the growing season, vigorous young shoots can ruin the lines of your bonsai style.

Use sharp pruning shears with short blades to nip long shoots throughout the growing season.

Shoot pruning

Prune the treetop severely on most species because of apical dominance; cutting back new shoots from three to five nodes to one or two nodes. If you start with a tree's lower branches, increase the number of nodes that you keep on a stem so the tree will keep some of its strength. The lowest branches should be the longest before pruning, since you will leave three to four internodes on the branch after pruning. Take fewer shoots off the lower branches, which grow more slowly. New shoots will arise from further back on the branch. These shoots will have shorter distances between leaf nodes and will give the tree an ancient twiggy appearance. Hold the shoot in one hand and with the other, snip off the excess vegetation above a leaf or bud. Use sharp scissors to cut stems above a node.

Cut back vigorous shoots to shrink space between leaf nodes. Cut slightly above the leaf petiole.

Bud pruning

Pinch terminal buds of elm, maple, and zelkova in early spring to encourage a fine network of branches. After shoot pruning various maples, buds appear not only at leaf nodes but also on trunk and branches. Left alone, excess buds may open, generating unwanted branches and more pruning, which could mar the bonsai. Remove excess buds by rubbing them off with your fingers or plucking them off with tweezers.

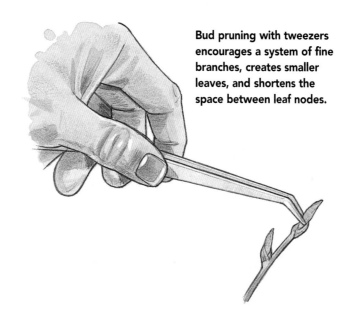

Bud pruning with tweezers encourages a system of fine branches, creates smaller leaves, and shortens the space between leaf nodes.

Branch pruning

During a temperate tree's winter dormancy, take off branches that grow too long for the shape of the tree. For most styles, the ultimate shape of the bonsai is some type of triangle. Throughout the growing season, trim back any new growth that upsets the balance of your bonsai's desired shape. To remove a secondary branch from a main one or from the trunk, hold the branch steady with one hand and use a concave branch cutter to remove the unwanted branch from the trunk. A concave cutter scoops subsurface tissue so that the healed wound is flush with the tree's outline. (Shears, saws, and other pruning tools that make flat cuts produce a raised mass at the wound site, interrupting the contour of the trunk.) After pruning, use a sealant to mask the fresh cut. Ideally, the shape of the final vertical cut will promote quicker healing because rising sap will reach the bark immediately over a cut, which doesn't happen with a horizontal cut.

Use a concave branch cutter to remove undesirable branches from the trunk or from a main branch.

Shaping Tools

COPPER, ALUMINUM, PLASTIC-COATED COPPER WIRE IN DIFFERENT GAUGES:

Shaping a bonsai usually requires some wiring of its trunk and branches. The kind of wire used depends on the grower's preference. Aluminum wire has a silvery appearance while anodized aluminum wire looks coppery and inconspicuous. Both aluminum and copper wire are flexible when applying them to bonsai but will harden with time. Copper hardens more than aluminum, which stays softer and may be less likely to damage the tree. Wire may have a plastic coating or be wrapped with paper or raffia to protect the bark as the wired tree grows. If you use aluminum wire (a good choice for beginners), work with a larger gauge wire. The finer gauge of copper required for the same job can cause more girdling than aluminum. Select wire one-third to one-half the width of the branch or trunk being bowed. Most trees need wire of two or three different gauges for complete shaping. Bonsai wire gauges range from 18 for delicate jobs to 8 for heavy trunks.

WIRE CUTTERS: As their name implies, wire cutters cut pieces of wire to wrap around bonsai trunks and branches. When training ends, you can use wire cutters to take the wire off styled trunks and branches. Do not unwind the wire from the branches. Instead, cut the wire off the tree at intervals of an inch to avoid damaging the branches. Some wire cutters look like pliers with a curving elongated handle, while others are scissors style.

WIRE BRUSH: Before shaping your bonsai, your tools must be clean and sharp. Wire brushes work well to remove rust from metal tools. In the process of making *jin* or *shari*, you can use wire brushes to refine and remove loose wood fibers from the deadwood surface.

JINNING PLIERS: You can use this tool to maneuver wire to shape a bonsai or to strip bark and deadwood, giving your bonsai an aged and weathered look. Its long jaws shut tight to clasp and bend

wire or to peel wood. Serrations on the jaw increase the tool's ability to grasp a branch or wire. Handles vary in length, the longer and heavier ones providing more force when manipulating wire or branches.

BRANCH BENDERS: Branch benders work with or without wire to add movement to tree parts. Benders have a jackscrew and vinyl-covered hooks that fit over a branch or trunk during alteration. They work progressively: every few days you tighten the central jackscrew a little until the hooked branch has the shape you desire. Leave the bender in place until the branch's new curve sets.

GRAVERS, STRAIGHT AND SPOON BENT: Bonsai growers carve *jin* and *shari* with gouges. Straight shank gouges work well on flat and easy-to-reach places. Gravers with spoon-bent shanks curve just before the blade. They can help you make contact with less-accessible areas.

LIME-SULFUR: Paint *jin* and *shari* yearly or more to preserve deadwood.

Wiring and Shaping Techniques

Wiring a root ball into a container can stabilize trees. Conifers and young trees in particular benefit from being wired into a bonsai dish.

Wire is useful in the process of growing bonsai. When potting or repotting, use looped wire to keep plastic mesh over drainage holes at the bottom of pots and then to anchor the tree's root ball in the bonsai dish. When styling your bonsai, wire becomes a critical asset. Once you have pruned your bonsai to its basic branches, you can begin to refine its shape according to the chosen style. Turning a tree into a bonsai may require reshaping with wire, ideally during dormancy for conifers and before bud break for deciduous trees. With care, however, you can wire most trees at any time. Wiring can change the direction of trunks and branches. After three months to a year, depending on the type of tree, cut the wire by starting at the tip rather than the base of trunks and branches. Do not harm the bark, twigs, or leaves when removing the wire.

Wiring a trunk into a container

During the initial potting up or early in the repotting process, you may need to stabilize your tree in its container by wiring it to the base. Many trees need stabilizing, especially conifers with their thick covering of rigid leaves that give little in the wind. To anchor a root ball, thread a long piece of wire beneath the dish and up through holes at either end of the dish. Bend the wire ends back outside the dish. Add a thin layer of potting mix and position the root ball in the dish. Tie the wire around the root ball at the back of the dish by twisting the ends together with pliers. The larger the dish, the more anchorage wires you may need both in front and in back of the root ball. Finish repotting by adding more soil and working it around the roots and leveling it with a potting trowel.

Reshaping a trunk with wire

First, cut a wire one-third longer than the job you need to accomplish. For a 12-inch trunk, cut a wire 16 inches long. Anchor the wire in the potting soil as deeply as you can along side the back of the trunk, and work upward from the tree base, winding from the trunk to a major branch. Make spiraling loops tilted to a 45-degree angle and separated by one-quarter inch or more of trunk. Tight wiring can harm the plant and loose wiring has little or no effect on changing the direction of growth. To keep the tree supple, cease watering a few days before wiring, since moisture makes a freshly watered tree turgid. Once you have wired the trunk, you can gently change its direction.

Wrap the wire so that it is neither tight nor loose.

Wiring and Shaping Techniques
(continued)

Thread wire up through the drainage holes to hold the root ball in place, twisting the ends together behind the tree.

Start wiring at the trunk near the base of the limb and spiral evenly along the branch from the bottom to the tip.

Reshaping branches

You can shape a tree's branches to look old and windswept or to improve the balance of the canopy. For example, wiring branches so that they slant down makes them look bent with age.

When you wire branches, start from the base of the trunk, moving up to the lowest main branch and spiraling outward toward the branch tip. Avoid crossing wire with more wire at any point since that can hurt the bark. Bend the branches lightly after wiring into the desired shaped. You may need to repeat the wiring process if the branches start to revert to their original shape. In that case, spiral the wire in the opposite direction to avoid grooving the bark.

Bad wiring is evident in this tree. The wire winds too closely in some areas and too far apart in others.

The wire on these branches varies in size. Gauge depends on the size of the trunk and each branch being shaped.

Sharimiki, the driftwood technique, adds drama to a juniper's contorted trunk.

Deadwood techniques

Because the appearance of age is desirable, bonsai growers work hard to make their trees look old. They use the advanced deadwood techniques of *jin*, *shari*, *sharimiki*, and *sabamiki* to age their trees before beginning the wiring process. In nature, trees that exhibit these extreme weathering effects survive on mountains. *Jin* may simulate either a dead branch stub years after a snowstorm that broke it or a tree struck by lightning with its top destroyed, leaving a bare stub at its apex. The size of the *jin* depends on the size of tree, with big trees having longer *jin* than trees that are slight. While *jin* affects branches, *shari* deadens part of a tree trunk. *Shari* is useful for disguising pruning scars on the front of the trunk. Use *jin* and *shari*, the most common deadwood techniques, on all conifers and some deciduous trees. It may take several seasons or years to produce successful results. *Sharimiki*, the driftwood technique, is uncommon and theatrical. Typically a deadwood yew or juniper, this bonsai is bare of all but a few stripes of live bark supporting a few live branches. *Sabamiki*, the hollow-trunk style, may be used on an evergreen or deciduous tree with part of its trunk hollowed to look ancient. *Sabamiki* can disguise a scarred trunk or front-facing branch that has been cut off.

A *sabamiki* trunk gives this bald cypress bonsai the appearance of great age.

For deadwood, use pliers to grasp loosened bark and pull it off.

Sharis **increase the feeling of age, movement, and weathering in this trunk.**

Wiring and Shaping Techniques
(continued)

Strip the branch of foliage and twigs and cut the end off, leaving a stub of suitable length.

Jin

■ To make *jin*, use an extra branch or a second (taller) leader on a tree.

■ Remove foliage and twigs from the branch and cut the end off, leaving a stub of the appropriate length.

■ Loosen bark around the base of the branch stub with a sharp knife or branch cutter.

■ Use *jinning* pliers to grasp and then strip the freed bark, starting at the branch base.

■ With the pliers, clasp slivers of wood at the top of the stub and strip away some of the white wood to expose the grain and shape the stub. You can shape the *jin* further with gouges.

■ With a wire brush, clean unwanted remnants of wood off the *jin*.

■ Paint the deadwood with a lime-sulfur blend to bleach and preserve the wood.

Use a wood chisel or sharp knife to loosen the bark. Then grasp and remove the bark with pliers to expose the grain.

Paint the deadwood with a lime-sulfur blend to preserve it and to lighten its color.

ROCK PLANTING

Rock plantings evoke natural crags, eroded boulders, and islands jutting from lakes. They symbolize survival against the odds. These plantings take two principal forms. In clinging-to-rock bonsai, tree roots make no contact with the soil in the dish. Instead, they grow in tiny peat or soil-filled crevices and pockets in a rock that sits in a flat dish of sand or water. The other type, root-over-rock bonsai, has roots that grow around a rock and reach into the dish. This style represents a tree once rooted in soil over an underground boulder. Time and weather have eroded the soil, leaving the rock and root tops exposed and the bottoms still in the soil. Both styles of rock plantings make spectacular landscape vignettes.

Root-over-rock style suits many plants, including Japanese maple *(Acer palmatum)*, elm *(Ulmus)*, fig *(Ficus)*, serissa, and chrysanthemum. Look for an irregular hard rock like granite. Ideally, it will be up to 1 foot high with top-to-bottom ridges for holding young roots in place. Start with a cutting or seedling. Plant it in a deep, narrow bonsai pot to lengthen the roots. Wait a year before planting the tree on a rock. Slather a blend of peat, water, and fine clay or loam over the rock, especially in the crannies where you want roots to grow. Arrange the roots on the rock and coat them thickly with the peat paste. Wind sisal or lead wool over the roots and rock to secure but not hurt the roots. You can also glue short pieces of wire to the rock with epoxy cement to keep a root in place. Thicken and lengthen the roots by planting the tree and rock in a large pot, keeping the top of the roots exposed. During the next few years you can cultivate the trunk and branches. When the roots look more substantial, repot the tree with the rock uncovered and shape the crown. Don't let the roots dry out. Keep them damp by frequent misting. Protect the bonsai from frost since roots are particularly vulnerable when exposed.

Glue short pieces of wire to the rock with epoxy cement. Use the wire to hold roots in place on the rock.

Once the cement hardens and the wires are secure, affix planting mix to the rock, then wire the tree in place.

Caring
FOR YOUR BONSAI

Nurturing bonsai differs from cultivating in-ground trees. The shallow dish where a bonsai tree grows affects its hardiness and nutrient absorption. Temperate bonsai species live outdoors and must experience the seasons, often with some protection, to remain healthy. On the other hand, tropical plants lack cold hardiness and can survive only indoors in cold climates. In hot regions, however, tropicals may thrive indoors and out. Providing the right environment with adequate light, water, and air circulation is crucial to a bonsai's vitality. Although diseases are rare, knowing how to deal with them, or with insect problems if they occur, will ensure a vigorous old age for your bonsai.

Light

Whether you cultivate your bonsai indoors or outside, it needs light to grow. The amount, however, varies with the species. Most bonsai trees require full sun to part shade.

Place your outdoor bonsai dishes on raised benches, shelves, or tables installed above pet height for added safety. Before you arrange your bonsai area, look for microclimates that may affect plant growth. For example, if you site plants against a protected south-facing wall where the sun is intense, you may be able to raise plants from a warmer climate than your own. Watch the sun move across your property. Will the shadow of the house keep the sun off your plants?

The north side of the house is shady, so take that into account when placing your plants. If your garden, deck, patio, or balcony is in the shade, choose shade-tolerant plants. These include boxwood (*Buxus microphylla*), jade plant (*Crassula ovata*), ivy (*Hedera helix*), fig (*Ficus*), snow rose (*Serissa foetida*), and azalea (*Rhododendron*).

Even sun-loving plants need a little shade from time to time. After repotting bonsai trees, baby them for a few weeks by shielding them from strong sunlight. Afternoon shade may also help trees with sensitive leaves avoid browning and sun scorch. If you live in a hot, sunny climate, grow a tree that requires full sun in filtered or light shade. The heat of

Growing plants near a sunny brick wall creates a warm microclimate in your garden.

unobstructed sunlight can bake a root system in a shallow ceramic pot.

Trees grown indoors need abundant light, or growth may be leggy since light inside a building is not as strong as light outdoors. A south-facing window is ideal for sun-loving tropicals and subtropicals, particularly ones with fruit and flowers. Bonsai may also survive by windows on a building's east and west sides. Keep plants away from extremely hot window glass. To keep growth even on all sides, rotate bonsai about 90 degrees every few days. If possible, keep indoor bonsai outdoors during the summer, avoiding exposed locations where wind can damage them. When moving plants outside for the summer, set them first in a partly shaded, protected spot. After a few days, move them into a sunnier location and eventually into full sun. Reverse this process in fall when bringing plants indoors.

If you cannot provide indoor plants with enough natural light for healthy growth or if you change their location, they may drop their leaves. Plants need leaves to manufacture food. For situations with insufficient light, give bonsai 12 to 16 hours of artificial light each day. Fixtures with two 48-inch, 40-watt fluorescent tubes give sufficient light when hung 4–6 inches above the plants. You can also use special grow-lights. They are more expensive but concentrate on the visible light spectrum's red and blue ends, which foster photosynthesis and plant growth. Incandescent light does not work as well as fluorescent lamps or specialized grow-lights because it does not produce enough light at the spectrum's blue end, where much photosynthesis occurs.

Shade your bonsai:

- ■ If you have just repotted
- ■ If you have trees with sensitive leaves in the afternoon sun
- ■ If you live in a hot, dry, sunny climate

Fluorescent light supplements low indoor light levels to assist plant growth.

Most indoor bonsai require bright indirect light for best performance.

Temperature

An unheated greenhouse can protect your bonsai from deep winter frosts.

By their nature, all plants are outdoor plants. Their survival depends on whether you can meet their growth requirements. Most woody plants suitable for bonsai originate in temperate zones with cold winters. These plants go dormant when temperatures drop. Deciduous trees may color up in fall and lose their leaves. Hardy trees such as most maples, zelkova, beech, pine, and spruce need to live outdoors and experience the seasons crucial to their growth, although most need winter protection from hard frost in cold climates.

If you plan to leave trees outdoors, they should be hardy; tender species should be raised indoors or in a heated greenhouse. Recognize that even the hardiest tree, when grown in a shallow dish, is susceptible to root damage when exposed to extreme heat, severe winds, and deep frost. Protect your trees in winter by placing them in a shed or garage during the winter months. Avoid subjecting your bonsai to drastic variations in temperature by ventilating the plastic and keeping them out of direct sunlight. In less frigid climates, bury the pot and roots in the ground or in a bed of fast-draining mulch. Maintaining the trees at 32–40° F ensures their safety. For summer protection in hot regions of the country, shield trees from desiccation by growing them in light shade.

If you raise tropical or subtropical bonsai indoors, keep them away from heating vents that can leave them parched. Locating bonsai too close to glass can also overheat your plants, dehydrating the fine efficient roots that absorb water and nutrients from the soil. Avoid setting tropical plants next to drafty glass doors and windows that create frigid winter microclimates. Likewise, keep plants away from television sets, computers, refrigerators, and other large appliances that release heat when they are plugged in and working.

Guard indoor bonsai from:

■ Window glass, which can overheat in the sun
■ Drafty windows and doors
■ Heating vents
■ Appliances with heat exhausts

Grown above ground, roots of temperate bonsai need winter frost protection. Bark mulch protects these roots from frost.

Humidity

Humidity measures water vapor in the air. Cold air holds less moisture than warm air, so an indoor plant may show signs of dehydration when temperatures drop. Humid air helps your bonsai retain moisture. If you cultivate raised-root bonsai or rock plantings, moisture in the air is crucial to their survival because exposed roots dry out quickly. Display hardy bonsai in these styles outdoors in an area protected from intense midday sunlight and drying gusts of wind. Setting a group of bonsai on trays of moist pebbles can help indoors, but it is questionable whether these trays will have the same effect outside and in the open air. Always keep space between the bottom of the bonsai container and the top of the water so that any roots touching the soil do not become waterlogged and rot.

Tropical and subtropical bonsai grown indoors live in your home's relatively arid conditions. Central heating dries the air while it warms the house. To measure the humidity level in a room, buy a gauge at a hardware or electronics store. Many of these tools tell you when the humidity is low, average, or high as well as giving you a numerical readout. High humidity may cause condensation on your window, whereas low humidity may cause plant leaves to wilt. There are several ways to increase the moisture content of the air inside your house when humidity is low. You can attach a humidifier to a forced-air furnace to increase moisture levels throughout the

whole house, or you can install individual cool-mist humidifiers in specific rooms where you grow bonsai.

Setting grouped plants on trays of damp pebbles has a similar but less-effective result. Bonsai specialists sell round, oval, and rectangular plastic or ceramic humidity trays, along with river pebbles to raise the pot out of water. Other choices are to keep wet sand, gravel, or clay pellets in the tray. Another form of humidity tray is a shallow plastic rectangle inset with a grid. When you water your bonsai, which sits on the grid, excess water gathers in the tray below. As the tray water

evaporates, it counteracts the loss of moisture from the foliage, which occurs during transpiration. The trays, many of which have tiny feet that raise them, also help protect indoor furniture from stains and watermarks.

Make more moisture

■ Attach a whole-house humidifier to your home's heating system
■ Install portable cool-mist humidifiers room by room
■ Set grouped plants on humidity trays of damp sand, pebbles, or gravel

Setting groups of indoor bonsai on trays of damp gravel may humidify the air around them.

Watering

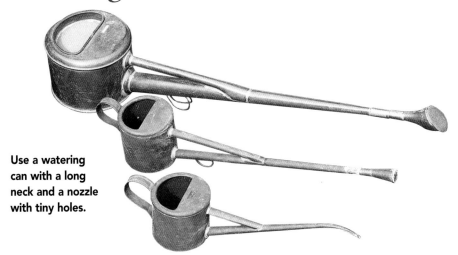

Use a watering can with a long neck and a nozzle with tiny holes.

Water outdoor bonsai when the soil feels dry to the touch.

Your bonsai needs enough water to keep it healthy, but the amount will vary by plant type, soil composition, location, pot shape, sun exposure, and time of year.

How do you decide when it is time to water a tree? You can check the soil in several ways. Lift your bonsai after you have watered it and excess moisture has drained away. Feel its weight in your hands. Wait a day or two; then lift the container and compare its weight to that of the preceding one. A dry container will feel light, but when fully watered, it will be heavy by comparison. Learn to recognize the different weights, because you must never let your bonsai completely dry out.

Other methods of detecting dryness exist. Keep a toothpick stuck in the soil about an inch from the edge of the container to use as a moisture gauge. Pull the toothpick out to see if the soil is dry and needs watering. If the toothpick is moist, you can wait. If the wood is dry, replace it in the soil, and water the plant thoroughly.

Your watering schedule will change from summer to winter. In winter, hardy bonsai trees need little water. Before you put them into their protected winter location, give them a thorough soaking. When a tree kept in a shed, garage, or unheated greenhouse looks dry, check the soil. It should be slightly moist. If it is not, water it. If you live in a place with adequate snow cover, you can heel the pot in the ground before it freezes, cover the lower trunk and branches with bark mulch, and encase it in snow after the first snowfall. During a thaw, check the soil for dryness. Water it when necessary.

Bonsai need frequent watering during the growing season. Starting in spring when trees break dormancy and their buds begin to swell, increase the amount of water you give them. Water most bonsai once a day while they actively grow. On very hot dry days, you may need to water more than once.

Several factors determine the frequency of watering. Trees growing on a rock or slab in sandy potting mix will dry out faster and thus need more frequent watering than trees growing in a pot with a richer soil mix. Trees grown on a site exposed to full sun, heat, and strong winds also dry out fast because of the increased rate of transpiration from the leaves. Conversely, trees growing in a somewhat shaded, protected spot retain more moisture. With other factors being equal, the soil in a deep container stays damp longer than soil in a shallow drum. A humid atmosphere also improves the soil's ability to retain moisture.

Dainty *mame* bonsai, which grow just 2–6 inches high, also require abundant watering. These are often young vigorous trees that will eventually become larger bonsai. *Mame* pots can be as small as 1 inch high and wide. With so little soil, plants require water several times a day at summer's peak. Group several indoor *mame* pots together on a tray of damp sand or gravel to

If a bonsai starts to wilt, immerse the pot in water until the soil stops bubbling.

In a rainstorm, tilt the bonsai dish to dispel excess water from roots.

increase the humidity around them and thus their ability to hold crucial moisture.

Water a bonsai tree until liquid runs out the drainage holes. Five minutes later, repeat. The flowing water forces stale air out of the pot and draws in fresh air as the water moves from the top to the bottom of the container. The best time to water is late afternoon, but early enough so foliage dries before dark. Use a watering can that has a long slender spout and a rose with fine holes. If you use tap water, let it sit overnight so that the water is at room temperature and the chemical additives have mostly evaporated. Hard water can leave mineral deposits on the soil. All your pots should be easy to reach with a hose or a watering can. Do not set plants in saucers full of drained water.

Do not underwater or overwater your bonsai since both can kill the plant. Fine feeder roots absorb water and nutrients from the soil. If there is too little water, they can dry out completely, causing the death of the tree. With too much water, the roots become oxygen deprived, rot develops, and the tree cannot survive. For drainage, make sure that bonsai containers have feet that raise them above the tray on which they sit.

Water often:

■ Trees trained in rock-growing styles
■ *Mame* bonsai
■ Trees in exposed sites

Mame bonsai need watering frequently since their root zones are extremely limited.

Fertilizing

Healthy bonsai trees eat well. Fine root hairs in the soil take up mineral nutrients, which mix with water and carbon dioxide to make food for the tree. Bonsai soil is intentionally porous, so the trees need frequent watering. Water flows through the soil, bringing fresh oxygen to the roots but washing away vital nutrients at the same time. Regular fertilizing replaces lost nutrients and keeps your bonsai fit, so leaves grow lush and trunks broad.

The three main elements of fertilizer are nitrogen (N), phosphorus (P), and potassium (K). Other elements such as calcium, magnesium, manganese, zinc, and copper appear in lesser quantities along with other micronutrients. Nitrogen supports strong leaf and plant growth. Dried blood is an organic nitrogen source. Phosphorus, or phosphate, increases flowering and fruiting. Bonemeal is high in phosphorus. Potassium, or potash, helps roots grow strong by managing the movement of nutrients from roots to foliage and of sugars from leaves to roots. Manures, especially poultry manures, are rich in potash.

Organic fertilizers include natural products like manure, bonemeal, dried blood, seaweed, and fish emulsion. Inorganic fertilizers produced from chemicals are usually more durable and concentrated than organic fertilizers. Both come in solid and liquid forms. The product you choose is not as important as using it correctly and in a timely way.

Your bonsai tree does not know the difference between organic and inorganic fertilizers since root hairs take in nutrients only in an inorganic, water-soluble state. Nutrients in an inorganic fertilizer are thus ready to use right away, but nutrients in organic fertilizers must first decompose into inorganic elements before the roots absorb them.

This naturally slow release of nutrients makes organic fertilizers milder and less likely to burn or harm a plant. Organic products contain numerous micronutrients that promote plant health and further the growth of beneficial bacteria and micorrhizal fungi, which increase a bonsai's resistance to stress and disease in the inert soil mixes preferred by many bonsai growers. On the downside, specialized organic bonsai fertilizers from Japan are hard to find in local stores and expensive to buy when you locate them. Inorganic fertilizers are widely available at nurseries, supermarkets, discount stores, and garden centers. They are often cheap and, when used according to package directions, effective. Moreover, their nutrients are accessible to plants with no delay. Disadvantages include the potential for burning a plant when you apply too much fertilizer or use it too near the plant's roots. Chemical imbalances occur when repeated overdoses of inorganic fertilizer create lethal amounts of salt compounds in the soil.

Apply liquid fertilizer to most bonsai from spring to the end of summer.

Scatter fertilizer pellets or granules all over the soil surface. Big fertilizer cakes go halfway between the trunk and the dish's edge.

TYPES OF FERTILIZER

INORGANIC GRANULES
- Easy to use: scatter on soil surface.
- Slow-release form is long-lasting.
- Relatively inexpensive and all-purpose.
- Can cause root burn when mixed in soil unless slow-release.

INORGANIC LIQUID
- Easy to use: dilute and pour. Inexpensive.
- All-purpose.
- Use every two weeks.
- Root burn occurs with inadequate dilution.

ORGANIC BLOCKS
- The traditional Japanese bonsai fertilizer.
- Set on top of soil halfway between trunk and edge of dish.
- Use wire or plastic-mesh fertilizer cups to keep cakes in place.
- Plastic cups also protect the cakes from hungry birds and other pests.
- Block formulation varies from 100 percent rapeseed to mixes including 50 percent fishmeal and 50 percent rapeseed; or 55 percent rapeseed or cottonseed meal, 30 percent bonemeal, 15 percent fishmeal.
- Long-lasting.
- Unattractive chunks 1 inch or larger.
- Sometimes appealing to flies.
- Can obstruct drainage during heavy rainfall.

ORGANIC PELLETS
- Scatter on soil surface.
- Apply to soil surface once in spring and again in midsummer.
- Nutrients wash into soil with each watering.
- They last so long they can grow moldy.

ORGANIC LIQUID
- Fish emulsion is mild, will not burn roots.
- Seaweed extract also good for foliar spray. Sometimes blended with fish emulsion.
- Use every two weeks.

The nutrient needs of your bonsai vary with the tree type, the time of year, and the age of your tree. Young bonsai trees require more fertilizer than old trees, and trees that grow fast need more food than slow-growing trees. Nitrogen needs peak in spring and early summer, while phosphorus and potassium take on greater importance as the growing season progresses. Because evergreens do not go fully dormant, you can fertilize them from early spring to early winter, whereas you would fertilize most deciduous trees from midspring to midfall. Do not feed your bonsai before repotting it, and wait a month after repotting to restart your fertilizing program.

Fertilizer facts

- Fertilize your bonsai regularly for lush leaves and ample trunk growth.
- Feeding requirements vary with the time of year and the tree's age and type.
- No matter which fertilizer you use, never exceed the amount recommended on the package label.

Seasonal Care

The following list will help you keep track of various seasonal tasks that you should take care of during the bonsai year.

Winter

■ Let your bonsai go dormant outside. Once your tree is dormant and the outdoor temperature reaches 15–20° F, move it into its winter shelter, which should have a constant temperature of 32° to 40° F. Frozen soil expands in the pot, which can break from the pressure.

■ Keep bonsai sheltered from extreme cold and wind. Because a bonsai tree lives in a shallow dish, its roots are fragile. Frigid air and strong winds can cause winterkill. Move trees to a protected spot such as a shelf in a shed or garage or a bench in a cool, unheated greenhouse. Bonsai need no light because they are dormant.

■ Water bonsai thoroughly before moving them to their winter location.

■ If you live where snowfall is reliably heavy, set plants into the ground before the earth freezes, and mulch the pot and lower branches with bark. Once it starts snowing, keep them covered with snow until spring. Protect buried pots from wind. During extended thaws, check bonsai to see if they need watering. If they do, water thoroughly and reapply mulch.

■ Spray trees with fungicide and insecticide to eliminate overwintering spores and insects that may overwinter in the soil or on your dormant bonsai trees.

■ Graft conifers and other evergreen shrubs and trees.

■ Test soil for dryness. If soil feels dry, water until moist, but avoid overwatering.

■ Prune heavy branches of most deciduous trees and evergreens toward the end of the winter.

■ Do not prune maples (*Acer*) and pines (*Pinus*).

■ Do not fertilize temperate or tropical bonsai.

■ Wire and shape trees.

■ Consult your notes to determine which plants need repotting in early spring. The older the tree, the less frequently you have to repot it since the roots of very old trees grow more slowly than those of young trees.

■ Stratify spring-sown seeds.

Spring

■ Repot and root prune most trees in early spring when

Wire evergreens in winter, wire deciduous trees before bud break in late winter or early spring.

they start to emerge from dormancy. Do this before the first shoots appear and until the first leaves develop.

■ Start fertilizing evergreens in early spring.

■ Fertilize tropicals and subtropicals with liquid fertilizer every two weeks. Dilute if internodes lengthen.

■ Prune conifers, which produce growth later, from now until the beginning of the summer.

■ Prune branches now for quick healing.

■ Spray trees with fungicide and insecticide before taking them outdoors for the growing season.

■ Continue to stratify seed.

■ Sow stratified seeds up to early May.

■ Wire and shape trees.

■ With permission, dig trees from the wild, keeping as much of the roots as possible.

■ Start fertilizing deciduous trees that have not been repotted in midspring. (Repotted trees need to re-establish themselves before you apply fertilizer.) Apply balanced liquid fertilizer every two weeks, starting in midspring after new leaves

Check bonsai trees regularly for signs of pests or diseases.

have hardened and continue until late summer. Make sure you dilute your plant food to the proper strength.

■ Wait to fertilize spring-flowering trees until after flowers have dropped. Applying fertilizer too quickly can keep fruit from growing.

■ Clean the plant shed or greenhouse once you have removed the bonsai.

■ In late spring, remove sheltered trees that were repotted in early spring.

■ Take evergreen cuttings.

■ Finish sowing seed before the end of May.

■ By the end of May, water trees once a day.

■ With thumb and forefinger pinch back long shoots of deciduous trees.

■ If frost is predicted, shelter trees that need protection.

Summer

■ Repot conifers, except pines, before they begin forming new shoots.

■ Move bonsai to summer sites. Set most trees in sunny, protected sites.

■ Water trees regularly. In hot weather, water at least once a day, depending on the plant's requirements.

■ If you are planning a vacation, arrange for a reliable friend to water your trees daily while you are away.

■ Using moss as a groundcover helps reduce evaporation when watering. Besides keeping the moss slightly damp, you can also set the pot in the shade and water late in the day to help your bonsai retain moisture.

■ Candle pines *(Pinus)*.

■ Fertilize trees. Slow-growing conifers need less fertilizer than fast-growing deciduous trees, so plan your

fertilizing schedule according to the tree's specific needs.

■ Rotate bonsai when necessary to encourage the appearance of even growth.

■ Check for insects on the soil, trunk, and both sides of the leaves. Treat insects when necessary for plant health.

■ Take softwood cuttings from trees like Japanese maples *(Acer palmatum)* and zelkovas *(Zelkova serrata)* to propagate more trees.

■ Pot up seedlings that you sowed in March.

■ Wire and shape trees.

■ Leaf prune deciduous trees such as beech *(Fagus)*, maple *(Acer)*, and sycamore *(Platanus)* to create smaller foliage. Do this from early summer until midsummer.

■ Pinch new shoots to keep trees shapely.

■ Give maples *(Acer)* and beeches *(Fagus)* a half-day of sun during the hottest part of the summer.

■ In late summer, start pruning pines.

Fall

■ Expose your hardy bonsai to the first frosts of autumn.

■ Protect tropical and subtropical species from frost.

■ Keep watering regularly through September. Stop by the end of October.

■ Reduce the frequency of plant feeding in September.

■ Stop feeding trees by midseason.

■ Repot pines *(Pinus)*.

■ Prune pines until the end of October.

■ Prune Japanese maples *(Acer palmatum)* in late November or early December after the sap stops rising.

■ Wire and shape conifers.

■ Destroy diseased fallen foliage and branches.

Prune conifers from early spring to early summer.

Repot most trees in early spring as they emerge from dormancy.

Bonsai Problem Solver

Some Japanese bonsai live more than 1000 years, a good indication of their health and vitality. Your bonsai will thrive if you care for your plants by examining their roots when transplanting and their leaves and trunks when watering and enjoying them day to day. In fact, the more time you spend with your bonsai, the better you will know when to water, fertilize, prune, and repot it, and the more vigorous it will be. You can grow bonsai for many years without encountering the following problems, but a pest infestation or a disease can happen. If it does, take the following cultural or chemical steps to help your plant regain its health. Note: Where possible, use cultural controls to deal with problems. Whether you choose organic controls such as *Bacillus thuringiensis* (Bt), neem oil, rotenone, pyrethrin, liquid copper, Bordeaux mix, or synthetic chemical products, do exactly as specified on the label and keep the product and treated plants away from pets, children, and wildlife. Ask a trusted nursery worker or extension agent about suitable synthetic chemicals for pest and disease control.

APHIDS

Tiny (⅛-inch) green, yellow, black, brownish, or gray soft-bodied insects cluster on the bark, leaves, or buds and suck the juice from the plant. Leaves may be discolored, curled, distorted, coated with a shiny or sticky substance, or drop off. A severe infestation of bark aphids may cause branches to die. Aphids are unable to digest fully all the sugar in the plant sap. They excrete the excess in a fluid called honeydew, which often drops below the tree or shrub. Ants feed on this sticky substance and are often present where there is an aphid infestation. A sooty mold fungus may develop on the honeydew, causing the leaves to appear black and dirty. Aphids are prolific, and populations can rapidly build up to damaging numbers on houseplants.

WOOLY APHIDS: Closely related to aphids, the adults are always covered with dense white filaments of wax. When this substance is removed, the insects appear purplish or green. Some species of these wooly "aphids" spend part of their lives on evergreens other than pines (usually spruces), often producing galls on the branches. In early summer, the insects migrate to pines and suck sap from the needles. Other species spend their entire lives on pines, feeding and reproducing on the trunks. Those species that spend the winter on other plants produce a generation in the fall that flies to the winter host.

Knock aphids off plants with a water jet. Spray aphids and wooly aphids on woody ornamentals and houseplants with insecticidal soap. If they persist, spray with neem or pyrethrin. Respray if the plant becomes reinfested. Follow label directions with care.

When aphids suck the juice from a plant, they excrete excess fluid called honeydew.

ANTS

Ants may not harm your bonsai trees, but a swarm on or below your plants can indicate that your trees have a problem with sap-sucking insects. Ants eat the honeydew that sucking insects secrete when they draw the juice from the leaves, trunks, or branches of your plants. Honeydew falls on the surface of the soil, where ants congregate to eat it. They also tap honeydew directly from the bodies of sap-sucking aphids and scales massed on plants.

Sometimes ants eat the sap dripping from peeled tree bark. On other occasions, they visit flowers and trees to gather nectar from glands at the base of leaves and buds. Raising your bonsai off the ground on a shelf or stand discourages ants by making your plants harder to access.

Ants are usually harmless but may indicate that other serious pests are present on your plant.

BEETLES

Beetles are shiny or dull hard-bodied insects with tough, leathery wing covers, which meet in the midback and form a straight line down the body. These insects consume leaf tissue, leaving it chewed, notched, or eaten between the veins. The damage makes the leaves appear lacy. Beetles may also chew flowers and bark, leaving holes in branches or the trunk.

Many different species of beetle feed on ornamental trees and shrubs. In most cases, both larvae (grubs) and adults feed on plants, often causing severe damage. The insects spend the winter as grubs inside the plants or in the soil. Adults winter in bark crevices or in hiding places on the ground. Adult beetles lay eggs on the plants or on the soil during the growing season. Depending on the species, the grubs may feed on foliage, mine inside the leaves, bore into stems or branches, or feed on roots. Beetle damage to leaves rarely kills the plant. Grubs feeding inside the wood or underground often kill branches or the whole plant.

Control measures usually focus on adult beetles. Remove beetles from the plant by hand in the morning and drown them in soapy water. Several insecticides also control these pests. Read the label carefully to find your plant listed there.

Beetles destroy leaf tissue, leaving it with a lacy appearance.

CATERPILLARS

Many caterpillar species feed on the leaves of trees and shrubs. From early spring to midsummer, female moths lay the eggs from which the caterpillars hatch; the time depends on the species. The larvae that hatch from these eggs feed singly or in groups on buds, on one leaf surface or the other, or on entire leaves. Certain caterpillars web leaves together as they feed. In some years, damage is minimal because of environmental conditions unfavorable to the pest or control by predators and parasites. However, when conditions are favorable, entire plants may be defoliated by late summer. Defoliation weakens plants because no leaves remain to produce food. When heavy infestations occur several years in a row, branches or entire plants may be killed.

When damage is first noticed, spray with an insecticide containing *Bacillus thuringiensis* var. *kurstaki* (Btk). Spray the leaves thoroughly. Respray immediately if the plant becomes reinfested.

Treat caterpillars when you first notice them causing damage.

Bonsai Problem Solver
(continued)

Lacebugs cause leaf spotting by sucking sap from the undersurface of leaves.

Leaf rollers feed within rolled leaves that they tie together with cobweb.

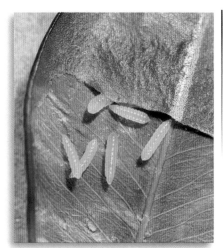

Leaf miners leave trails or dead patches that stand out against green leaves.

LACEBUGS

These insects cause spotting of leaves. Leaf spots may be brownish, yellow, white, or completely discolored. Sometimes the insects are visible, feeding on the topsides or undersides of the leaves. These insects can be controlled with various insecticides. For example, sycamore lacebugs survive the winter as adults in bark crevices or other protected areas on the tree. When buds open in the spring, adult females use a brown sticky substance to attach their eggs to the undersides of leaves. When eggs hatch, the spiny, wingless, immature insects and later the brown lacy-winged adults suck sap from the undersurfaces of the foliage. The green leaf pigment disappears, resulting in the characteristic white and green mottling. As the lacebugs feed, droplets of brown excrement accumulate around them.

When damage appears in spring, spray young trees with insecticidal soap. For more serious cases, spray with summer oil or a chemical insecticide. Cover the undersurfaces of the leaves thoroughly. Repeat 7–10 days later. Early spraying is essential to damage prevention.

LEAF ROLLERS

Leaves are rolled, usually lengthwise, and held together with cobweb. The rolled leaves are chewed. When a rolled leaf is opened, a green caterpillar ½ to ¾ inch long may be found feeding inside. Flower buds may also be chewed. Leaf rollers are the larvae of small (up to ¾ inch), brownish moths. The insects spend the winter as eggs or larvae on a plant. In the spring the larvae feed on the young foliage, sometimes tunneling into and mining the leaf first. They roll one or more leaves around themselves, tying the leaves together with silken webbing, then feed within the rolled leaves. This provides protection from weather, parasites, and chemical sprays. In the fall, the larvae either mature into moths and lay the over-wintering eggs or spend the winter inside the rolled leaves.

In the spring, when leaf damage is first noticed, spray with Btk or an insecticide. For the insecticide to be most effective, apply it before the larvae are protected inside the rolled leaves. In the spring, check plants periodically for the first signs of leaf roller infestation.

LEAF MINERS

Leaf miners are the larvae of flies, moths, beetles, or sawflies. The adult female moths lay their eggs on or inside the leaves, usually in early to late spring. The emerging larvae feed between the leaf surfaces, producing green or whitish translucent blisters, blotches, or winding trails, which stand out prominently against normal green foliage. The insects pupate inside the leaves or in the soil and emerge as adults. Some adults also feed on the leaves, chewing holes or notches in them. Tearing open an infested leaf will reveal one to several small green, yellowish, or whitish insects.

Control of leaf miners is difficult because they spend most of their lives protected inside the leaves. Ask your local cooperative extension office when the adults are emerging in your area. Spray adult leaf miners with an insecticide. Buy only products that list your plant on the label and follow label directions.

RED SPIDER MITES

Spider mites suck sap from the leaves and buds of infested plants. As a result, green leaf pigment (chlorophyll) disappears, leaving sickly yellowish stipples. While feeding on leaves and stems, mites produce fine webbing that collects dust and dirt. New growth looks distorted. To see if spider mites are infesting your plant, hold white paper underneath an affected branch and tap the branch sharply. If green, red, brown, or yellow specks drop to the paper and crawl around, they are mites. Some are active in a growing season with warm, dry weather. Others, especially those infesting conifers, prefer cooler weather and are active in spring, fall, and winter during warm spells and in mild-winter climates. At the onset of hot weather, these mites cause maximum damage. Mites affect spruce, holly, juniper, and fruit and nut trees. When you first see damage, spray plants with water, insecticidal soap, neem, or a miticide. Buy only products that list your plant on the label and follow label directions.

Red, brown, green, or yellow spider mites infest many species of tree.

ROOT NEMATODES

Root nematodes are microscopic worms living in soil. Symptoms of infestation include premature drop of small discolored leaves, twig and branch dieback, and declining plant health. While some varieties are beneficial, others feed on plant roots. This damages, stunts, or enlarges roots so they cannot supply water and nutrients to aboveground plant parts. Affected plants grow stunted or slowly die. Nematodes are prevalent in the South in moist, sandy loam. They move a few inches each year but may be carried long distances by soil, water, dirty tools, or infested plants. Laboratory testing will confirm the presence of nematodes. Contact the local extension office for sampling instructions and addresses of testing laboratories. Poor soil structure, drought stress, overwatering, nutrient deficiency, and root rot produce symptoms similar to nematode decline. Eliminate these problems as causes before sending soil and root samples for testing. To keep your bonsai healthy, mulch, water, and fertilize to minimize your plant's stress. Repot often to control the presence of nematodes because chemicals to kill these pests are not available to the gardening public.

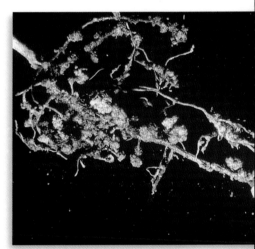

Root nematodes may cause swellings on roots, plant decline and death.

SCALES

Many plants, including fruit and nut trees, azalea and rhododendron, maple, ivy, houseplants, juniper, linden, and oak are subject to scales. They can cover leaves, stems, trunks, and branches with crusty or waxy bumps with soft undersides. Affected leaves turn yellow and may drop. Scales infest trees and shrubs. In spring to midsummer, the young settle on leaves, branches, or trunks to suck sap. Their legs wither and a shell develops over their bodies. Some species excrete excess sap sugar in a fluid called honeydew. Sometimes sooty mold develops on sticky honeydew, turning leaves black and dirty. An uncontrolled infestation of scales may kill a plant after two or three seasons. When the young are active, spray with summer oil or an insecticide. Contact your cooperative extension office for the best time to spray for scales in your area. The following spring, before new growth begins, spray trunk and branches with dormant oil to control over-wintering eggs and insects. Buy only products that list your plant on the label and follow label directions.

Untreated scale infestations can kill plants within three seasons.

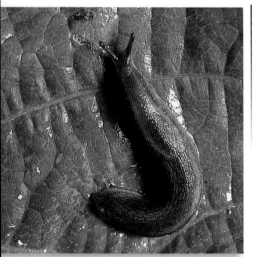

Slugs feed on leaves at night, leaving irregular holes with smooth edges.

SLUGS AND SNAILS

Slugs and snails feed on a variety of plants, leaving irregular holes with smooth edges in leaves or shearing them off entirely. Silvery trails wind around the plants and soil nearby. Snails and slugs move around and feed on rainy days or at night; check for them by inspecting your bonsai trees at night by flashlight. These pests are mollusks and need to be moist. They avoid direct sun and dry places, hiding under flowerpots or in thick groundcovers. Snails and slugs are similar, except that snails have hard shells. In protected places female slugs lay masses of white eggs encased in slime. Female snails bury their eggs in the soil or in a slimy mass. The young look like their parents, only smaller. To banish them, apply suitable bait around trees and shrubs you wish to protect. Before spreading bait, wet the area to encourage snail and slug activity that night. Saucers of beer buried to the rim in soil and leaves of cabbage draw snails and slugs. Collect the dead each morning. If you use chemical bait, repeat every two weeks as long as they are active.

Plants make galls in response to the presence of a foreign substance.

GALLS

Trees and shrubs sometimes develop galls, which are small or large bumps that look like part of the plant or pieces of fruit. Galls occur because a foreign substance has been injected into the tree. As a protective measure, the tree surrounds the substance with firm tissue. Most galls do no serious damage, but small plants may be stunted if the gall blocks the flow of nutrients. Galls are specific to the tree type and to the insect, bacterium, or fungus causing them. Oak, maple, camellia, azalea, and pine are susceptible. Insects cause most galls. Oak galls can appear on leaves, branches, or twigs. Leaf galls may result in discoloration and premature drop, and some twig galls may cause twig dieback. If insect galls cause a problem or if you do not like their looks, cut them off before adult insects emerge in spring. Destroy stems affected by bacterial crown gall below the galled area. Sterilize pruning shears with rubbing alcohol after each cut. If galls are unsightly, you may want to control the insects or diseases causing them. Take samples to a garden center, or consult an arborist.

Maple anthracnose causes leaf browning and defoliation.

MAPLE ANTHRACNOSE

Irregular, light brown spots of dead tissue on maple leaves from May to August may be maple anthracnose, particularly if spots occur along the veins in or after wet, humid weather. Dark spore-producing structures on leaf bottoms form while leaves are on the tree, and sunken reddish ovals appear on infected twigs. A fungus that winters on fallen leaves or in sunken cankers on the maple's twigs causes the disease. Rainy weather blows and splashes spores onto young leaves. Dead spots on leaves expand and cause defoliation. The tree grows new leaves if defoliation occurs in spring or early summer. When a tree is affected for successive years, the fungi can kill branches. Trees affected for one year do not need chemical control. Rake and destroy old leaves to help avoid reinfection. Pruning dead twigs below the canker on the bark may also reduce the amount of disease the following year. If the next spring is wet and humid, treat valuable specimens with a chemical fungicide or a Bordeaux mix. (Use carefully, as this mixture of copper sulfate, lime, and water can burn tree leaves in damp conditions.)

BLACK SPOT

A fungus causes black spot, a common rose disease that reduces flower quality and numbers in areas with rainy, humid springs and summers. Circular black spots with irregular edges appear on leaf tops in spring. Tissue around spots or whole leaves may yellow and infected leaves drop prematurely. Severely infected plants lose leaves by midsummer. Fungi winter on infected leaves and stems. Splashing water spreads spores from plant to plant, forming pinhead-size spots that enlarge up to ¾ inch in diameter as fungi spread. Spots may join to form blotches. Repeated infection kills plants. Spray with a mixture of baking soda, liquid soap, and warm water or with a chemical fungicide. Repeat the treatment at intervals of seven to 10 days while weather remains wet. Omit spraying during hot, dry spells in summer. Cut off infected stems. Avoid overhead watering. In fall, rake up and destroy fallen leaves. After pruning plants during the dormant season, spray with a lime-sulfur spray. The following spring, when new growth starts, begin the spraying program again. Plant resistant varieties.

Keep black spot in check by sterilizing gardening tools after each use.

CHLOROSIS

Chlorosis is the yellowing of foliage because of loss or breakdown of chlorophyll. Causes may be disease or infestation, poor growing conditions, or lack of nutrients. The newest leaves at the stem tips of trees, shrubs, and vines are most affected. Except in extreme cases, the veins of affected leaves and older leaves remain green while foliage turns pale green or yellow. Plants frequently suffer from deficiencies of iron and other trace nutrients such as manganese, magnesium, and zinc that are essential to normal plant growth. Although these nutrients may be present in fertilizer and potting mix, they are easily washed out with frequent watering. Moreover, potting soil that is alkaline or wet may cause nutrients to form compounds that cannot be used by plants. To correct iron deficiency, spray foliage with liquid iron and apply it to the soil around the plant. Apply ferrous sulfate or lime-sulfur spray to correct the pH. Reduce soil pH by adding acidic materials like peat to the soil mix when transplanting. Maintain an acidic pH by fertilizing with an azalea, camellia, and rhododendron food rated 10-7-7.

Chlorosis, or leaf yellowing, may result from an iron deficiency.

POWDERY MILDEW

A thin layer or irregular patches of grayish-white powdery material covering a bonsai's leaves, flowers, and young stems may indicate powdery mildew. Infected leaves may turn yellowish or reddish and drop. Some leaves or branches may be distorted. In late fall, tiny black dots (spore-producing bodies) sprinkle the white patches like ground pepper. Several fungi that thrive in both humid and dry weather cause this common disease. Some attack older leaves and plant parts; others attack young tissue. Plants growing in shady areas are often infected. Powdery patches consist of fungal strands and spores, which the wind spreads to healthy plants. Since powdery mildew attacks many plants, fungi from a diseased plant may infect other plants in the garden. Powdery mildew rarely causes permanent harm to plants. Control it by destroying infected leaves, by leaving adequate space between bonsai containers to improve air circulation and by growing mildew-resistant varieties. Bordeaux mix and other chemical fungicides may also control powdery mildew.

Plentiful air circulation between plants helps control powdery mildew.

Bonsai Problem Solver
(continued)

In wet heavy soils, wilt and root rot may destroy pine's roots and stems.

WILT AND ROOT ROT

Young leaves are yellowish and wilting. Eventually the whole plant dies even though the soil is moist. Dead leaves remain attached to the plant and are rolled along the midrib. The symptoms develop over a few weeks or take many months. The tissue under the bark near the soil is darkly discolored; to check for discoloration, peel back the bark at the bottom of the plant. A distinct boundary exists between white healthy wood and dark diseased wood. Several different soil-inhabiting fungi or water molds cause this disease in a variety of ornamentals, such as pines and camellias. They destroy the roots and may work their way up the stem, eventually killing the plant. Wet conditions favor the fungi, which are most common in heavy, poorly drained soils. Dry the soil out. Use a fast-draining soil mix and mound the soil in the pot to improve drainage. Grow plants resistant to wilt and root rot, including sasanqua camellia, Alaska cedar, Sawara cypress, Pfitzer's juniper, Savin juniper, dwarf mugho pine, Hiryu azalea, and America arborvitae. No chemical control is available.

Wind and splashing rain can spread rust spores to healthy plants.

RUST

The symptoms of rust are yellow, orange, red, or black powdery pustules that appear on topsides or undersides of leaves and, occasionally, on bark. The powdery material can be scraped or rubbed off. Leaves are discolored or mottled yellow to brown and may be twisted, distorted, dry, and then drop off. Infected stems may be swollen or blistered, or they may develop oblong or hornlike galls. Many different species of rust fungi infect coniferous and deciduous trees and shrubs. Wind and splashing water spread rust spores to healthy plants. When conditions are favorable (moist, with temperatures from 55° to 75° F), the spores germinate and infect the tissue. Some rust fungi are fairly harmless and do not require control measures. Destroy fallen leaves in autumn to keep rust from overwintering and spreading. Good air circulation helps prevent rust. When watering, keep moisture off the leaves of susceptible plants. Organic and chemical fungicides can also control rust.

Cedar-apple rust affects junipers and apple trees with different symptoms.

CEDAR-APPLE RUST

Most rusts attack one species or a few related species of plant. However, cedar-apple rust requires two species to complete its life cycle. It affects both juniper (*Juniperus*) and apple trees (*Malus*), alternating between the two with different symptoms. Wind-borne spores from apple or crab apple leaves infect juniper needles in summer. The fungi grow little until the following spring, when brownish green swellings or galls begin to form. The second spring, during warm rainy weather, orange jellylike "horns" grow from depressions in the galls. Wind carries spores from the horns to infect apple trees. By midsummer orange spots appear on apples and topsides of leaves. In August, spores are released and the wind carries them back to junipers. The cycle takes 18–20 months on juniper plus 4–6 months on apple. To deal with cedar-apple rust, remove galls and destroy them. When possible, keep junipers and apples several hundred yards apart. Spraying junipers with a suitable fungicide in August may help prevent new infections from apple trees.

CANKER AND DIEBACK

This fungal disease harms Norway and Colorado blue spruces. Brown dry needles on low branches drop immediately or remain attached to the tree for a year, but eventually the entire branch dies back. Amber-color pitch oozes from infected areas, becoming white as it dries. The infection may spread upward. Determine if the tree is infected by slicing bark on a dead branch where diseased and healthy tissue meet and looking for tiny black spore-producing bodies underneath. Fungal infection starts at a wound, killing the surrounding healthy tissue. Canker develops and expands through the wood in all directions. When it encircles a branch, the branch dies and needles turn brown. Trees more than 15 years old and weak or injured trees are most susceptible. Prune and destroy dying branches below infected areas or where branches meet the trunk. After each cut, sterilize pruning shears with rubbing alcohol. Do not prune during wet weather. Keep trees vigorous by sufficient watering during dry spells and by fertilizing.

To remove dead branches, cut into healthy wood below sick spots.

VIRUSES

Camellia yellow mottle-leaf virus sometimes infects this popular bonsai subject. Irregular yellow splotches of various sizes and shapes appear on a camellia's evergreen foliage. Some leaves may be entirely yellow. The uninfected leaf portions remain dark green. Colored flowers may have irregular white blotches, but white flowers show no symptoms. The disease is usually harmless although extensive leaf yellowing may indicate the plant's weakness and declining health. Grafting or propagating from infected plants transmits the virus. This usually occurs at the nursery that grew the plant. Sometimes the virus is intentionally transmitted to get variegated flowers. Yellowing results from suppression of green pigment (chlorophyll) development. Leaves produce less food, weakening the plant. Once the camellia is infected, no chemical can control the virus. Buy only healthy plants. Protect your camellias from hot sun. Grow them in rich, well-drained soil and apply acidic fertilizer.

Camellia yellow mottle-leaf virus can weaken plants but is usually harmless.

VERTICILLIUM WILT

Verticillium wilt makes leaves yellow at the edges, then brown and dry. Leaves may wilt in hot weather. New ones are stunted and yellow. Some infected trees recover; some die within months or over several seasons. Peel dying bark to look for streaks that are either dark or barely visible when exposed. The disease is caused by soil-dwelling fungi and affects many trees and shrubs, persisting on plant debris and in the soil. Contaminated seeds, plants, soil, and bonsai tools spread the disease. Fungi spread upward from roots to branches to trunk through water-conducting vessels, which become plugged. Plugging cuts water and nutrient flow to branches, causing wilt and discoloration. Isolate infected plants. Add fertilizer and water to stimulate vigorous growth. Remove dead wood. Do not remove branches where leaves have recently wilted since these may produce new leaves in three to four weeks or the next spring. Keep healthy bonsai away from infected plants and sterilize tools after each use. No chemical control is available.

Plugged tissues destroy water and nutrient flow, causing dieback in crown.

Bonsai Plant Profiles

Deadwood effects suit the California juniper, which is a slow-growing, long-lived native of the western United States.

To express the beauty of nature in miniature, bonsai requires appropriate plant material. Some plants lend themselves better than others to the bonsai art. In the Bonsai Plant Profiles, you will discover traditional trees used for centuries to make bonsai— various pines, junipers, Yezo spruce, flowering fruit trees, and Japanese maples. North American trees and shrubs that are easy to find and grow also appear on the list, as well as tropical and subtropical plants that meet the needs of indoor gardeners and apartment dwellers.

Each profile describes the featured plant's appearance and special features such as outstanding fall foliage or spring flowers. Other desirable characteristics include attractive fruit, beautiful bark, striking leaves, and multiple season interest. If a plant family contains more than one form suitable for bonsai, the portrait may highlight several varieties with appealing and distinctive traits. Many trees in the profiles are Asian bonsai classics available at local or mail-order nurseries. (You will find some reputable mail-order nurseries in the Resources section on pages 123–124.)

You will also learn botanical and common names and their pronunciation and the plant's relative hardiness. Where noted, United States Department of Agriculture (USDA) hardiness zones indicate the annual average minimum temperature the plant can tolerate when growing in nature. By definition, bonsai trees grow in shallow containers above the ground, making their roots particularly vulnerable to heat and frost. Consequently, they are less hardy than the USDA zone indicates and need winter protection. Generally, the hardiness zone given in the plant profiles designates the coldest temperature that the bonsai can tolerate with appropriate winter protection. By locating your hardiness zone on the map (see page 122), you can learn which trees are most likely to survive winter in your climate.

In addition to hardiness, you will find general cultivation guidelines, including whether to grow a specific plant indoors or outdoors, watering requirements, soil needs, appropriate light levels, feeding schedule, pruning needs, and any pests and diseases that may afflict it. Many trees develop quickly during their first 10 years of cultivation and will need more frequent repotting and more drastic pruning of roots and shoots. The profiles address repotting schedules, which vary from one to several years, depending upon the age and vigor of the tree. Tips on pruning and styling your bonsai also appear on the plant pages.

These flowering tropical bonsai trees can grow outdoors in summer in temperate climates.

Acer buergerianum
AY-ser burr-juh-ree-AY-num

TRIDENT MAPLE, THREE-TOOTHED MAPLE
Aceraceae

Trident maples, named for their leaves with three pointed lobes, make effective bonsai trees because they develop quickly and look attractive year-round. These vigorous, drought-resistant, deciduous small trees or big shrubs lend themselves to bonsai training. Dwarf forms and cultivars with variegated, tiny, rounded, or deeply cut lobes are popular with Asian growers but may be hard to find in North America. Specimens may have one or several stems. Trident maples must live outdoors.

SPECIAL FEATURES: A four-season tree with excellent bark and leaves.

FOLIAGE: Bronze new growth, glossy dark green leaves, bright red and orange fall color.

BARK: Orange, brown, and gray exfoliating plates on older trees give winter interest.

HARDINESS: USDA Zone 5 in the landscape. Trident maple needs early winter protection in a bonsai container since its fast-growing roots are prone to frost damage.

LIGHT: Full sun with midday shade in midsummer.

SOIL: Acid, fast-draining; use standard bonsai mix.

WATER: Needs daily watering during the growing season because roots have high water content.

FERTILIZER: Once leaves open, use liquid fertilizer every other week during spring and summer.

PRUNING: Cut back tips of new shoots in spring and summer, keeping two pairs of leaves on young trees and one pair of leaves on old trees. When two new shoots appear at each leaf node, remove the tip and keep only one pair of leaves per shoot. In that way, the crown develops a fine network of branches. Annual leaf cutting will keep leaves small.

REPOT: Every year in spring before buds open.

PESTS AND DISEASES: Trident maples are usually problem-free. When severely stressed, however, they may be susceptible to anthracnose, leaf spot, and powdery mildew. Maple pests include aphids, borers, scales, and whiteflies.

STYLES: Broom, group planting, raft, curved-trunk, and clump styles suit trident maple's upright growth habit. Root-over-rock style is particularly successful since the tree's characteristic vitality fosters speedy root enlargement.

Leaf pruning reduces foliage size and intensifies trident maple's fall color.

Acer palmatum
AY-ser pol-MAY-tum

JAPANESE MAPLE
Aceraceae

Japanese maple foliage resembles the palm of a hand with five fingerlike lobes. Fresh shoots can be green, red, or flushed with purple while older bark is an attractive gray. Although the species is green, cultivars produce leaves that vary from green to purple and variegated green and white. The texture of this classic bonsai subject depends upon the cultivar. Varieties with feathery, finely cut leaves have a delicate texture, while those with shallow lobes are medium-fine in appearance when compared with other bonsai trees. This small deciduous tree or big shrub grows slowly with a variable habit, or mode of growth. It belongs outdoors but cannot survive without winter protection in most of North America. Because it leafs out early, it is often subject to late frosts that can damage or kill the tree. Hundreds of *A. palmatum* varieties, including a number of dwarfs, exist.

SPECIAL FEATURES: Slow growing; foliage in various textures and colors; red, red-purple, red-orange stems; outstanding fall color; elegant habit.

This Japanese maple in the twin-trunk style looks graceful in or out of leaf.

HARDINESS: USDA Zone 5 or 6 in the landscape, depending on the variety. Winter protection is necessary.
LIGHT: Sun to light shade. Shade is important in the heat of summer, when hot sunlight can scorch leaves.
SOIL: Well-drained, slightly acid, high in organic matter; standard bonsai mix.

WATER: Once or twice a day during the growing season, depending on the heat, and when necessary in winter to prevent dessication.
FERTILIZER: Every other week with diluted liquid fertilizer during spring and summer.
PRUNING: Prune leaves of healthy trees in midsummer to reduce leaf size and intensify fall color. Pinch tips of new shoots regularly to maintain the style and, where desirable, to encourage a fine network of branches. Prune maple branches when sap is not rising, either late in the dormant season or in midsummer.

Cutleaf Japanese maple (*A. palmatum* 'Dissectum') in the cascade style needs a deep pot to balance the fall of the trunk. The finely cut leaves add delicacy to the bonsai's flowing habit.

Acer palmatum
AY-ser pol-MAY-tum

JAPANESE MAPLE *(continued)*
Aceraceae

REPOT: Every two to three years in spring before buds open. Trees less than 10 years old may need more frequent repotting.

PESTS AND DISEASES: Japanese maples are typically healthy. When stressed, however, they may be particularly susceptible to aphids and scale. Check upper and lower leaf surfaces frequently during the growing season to catch any problem before it becomes severe.

STYLES: Many bonsai styles fit the Japanese maple, including broom, group planting, raft, curved-trunk, twin-trunk, triple-trunk, cascade, semi-cascade, and clump styles.

CULTIVARS: 'Atropurpureum', purplish red leaves, an upright habit, and bright red fall color.

'Dissectum', cutleaf variety with a mounded habit, golden fall color, and an airy appearance.

'Butterfly', cutleaf cultivar with variegated foliage in pink and blue-green with white margins that turn magenta in fall.

'Kashima', dwarf with tiny red-edged leaves in spring, turning green in summer and yellow in autumn.

A red-leafed Japanese maple in the curved trunk style stands out amid numerous green-leafed trees.

Bougainvillea
Boo-gun-VILL-ee-uh

PAPERFLOWER, BOUGAINVILLEA
Nyctaginaceae

Bougainvillea is the choice for long-lasting, brilliant color. In hot climates, bougainvillea is evergreen and grows outdoors year round. In cool climates, bougainvillea loses most of its foliage, whether you cultivate it indoors or bring it outside for the summer. The varieties best suited to bonsai are thorny, tropical South American vines. Because of bougainvillea's vigor and flexibility, you can train it quickly and easily into a bonsai. Its common name, paperflower, refers not to its tiny, plentiful white flower trumpets but to the three showy, papery bracts encircling each bloom. Blossoming depends on short day length and temperature. Peak periods of bloom include late fall, winter, and early spring. Some cultivars flower intermittently through the year. When moving an indoor bougainvillea outdoors, wait until evening temperatures stay above 50°F, and set your container in dappled shade for a few days to give the leaves time to adapt and avoid sun scorch.

SPECIAL FEATURES: Bright, petallike bracts in fuchsia, red, yellow, orange, purple, and white appear at the ends of new shoots. Drought tolerant; salt tolerant.

HARDINESS: Zones 9–11

LIGHT: Bougainvillea prefers strong sunlight. Grow it outside when temperatures are higher than 50°F at night or keep it indoors where it will grow in a window with a southern or western exposure.

SOIL: Regular bonsai mix. Needs free-draining soil.

WATER: Water with restraint especially in winter and when forcing flowers. In early summer, withholding water until leaves start to wilt may trigger blooming when days are long, but wilting may also induce leaf drop. Overwatering leads to leaf drop and root rot.

FERTILIZER: Monthly from spring to fall with liquid fertilizer.

The pink bracts of *B. glabra* last from summer to fall.

PRUNING: Blooms on new growth at ends of shoots and in the leaf axils. Cut off fading flowers. Prune branches on vigorous plants almost any time of year, but seal wounds to deter rot. Old branches break easily so wire young flexible branches when possible.

REPOT: Before new growth begins in spring every two to four years, depending on whether you live in a hot climate where roots grow fast or a cool climate where growth is slower. Avoid radical root pruning since bougainvillea has a delicate root system.

PESTS AND DISEASES: Leaf spot, chlorosis from lack of iron or magnesium, aphids, and leaf cutters; whiteflies and spider mites indoors.

STYLES: Curved-trunk, root-linked, twin-trunk, triple-trunk, root-over-rock, cascade, semi-cascade

CULTIVARS: 'Raspberry Ice'—showy, repeat bloomer with intense fuchsia bracts and variegated leaves with wide creamy margins; slow growing.

'Pink Pixie'—dwarf plant with little pink bracts.

'Helen Johnson'—miniature with red bracts.

Buxus microphylla 'Compacta'
(also known as
'Kingsville Dwarf' boxwood)
BUCK-sus my-kroh-FILL-uh

Kingsville Dwarf boxwood is a broadleaf evergreen shrub with tiny leaves and a dense network of branches. Usually wider than it is tall, this box has attractive bark that looks old even in its youth. You can pinch and prune this easy-to-grow plant into shape, often without wiring. Boxwood, which can tolerate some drought, thrives outdoors or indoors—an unusual characteristic for temperate plants.

COMPACT LITTLELEAF BOXWOOD
Buxaceae

SPECIAL FEATURES: Tiny leaves stay green year-round; old-looking bark; grows indoors or outside.

HARDINESS: USDA Zone 6 with winter protection. 'Kingsville Dwarf' also grows well indoors.

LIGHT: Dappled sun to partial shade. Indoors, it not only lives near windows but also thrives in the dark inner rooms of the house.

SOIL: Thrives in well-drained acid soil. Plant in standard bonsai mix.

WATER: Water every one to two days as needed during the growing season, less in winter.

FERTILIZER: Feed liquid fertilizer every two weeks from spring when growth starts until late summer.

PRUNING: In spring or summer, open the crown and make branching more visible by cutting away some of the secondary inner branches. To maintain the style during the growing season, pinch or cut back shoots by half when they reach ½ inch long.

REPOT: Every two to three years. Avoid soggy soil by watering when almost dry.

PESTS AND DISEASES: Root rot may occur in overwatered plants. Also watch out for mites, scale, and leaf miners.

STYLES: Most styles. Suitable for *mame*.

CULTIVARS: 'Morris Midget', when unpruned forms a slow-growing, 1 foot high by 1½ foot wide mound of yellowish green, tiny leaves.

B. 'Green Gem' is a hardier hybrid more suited to northern outdoor bonsai. It has a spherical habit. Unpruned, it measures 2 feet by 2 feet at maturity.

'Kingsville Dwarf' box in the raised-root style thrives inside or outside the house.

Carpinus
Kar-PYE-nus

HORNBEAM
Betulaceae

Hornbeams are deciduous, upright trees notable for toughness and tolerance of urban conditions. Some species grow in the forest understory encircled by taller trees. Hornbeam's oval, toothed foliage can withstand the shade and humidity created by these crowded conditions. European hornbeam *(Carpinus betulus)* and American hornbeam *(C. caroliniana)* have muscled steel-gray bark and variable but appealing fall color. When trained as a bonsai, this deciduous tree grows outdoors but needs protection from hot summer sun and winter frost. The leaves, shaped like long ovals with pointed tips and toothed edges, are reminiscent of birch leaves. Korean hornbeam *(C. coreana)* makes an excellent bonsai plant because of its little leaves, short spaces between leaf nodes, and bright red-and-yellow striped fall color. Turkish hornbeam *(C. turczaninovii)* also has tiny leaves and excellent fall color. Because of their vigor, hornbeams are suited to many bonsai styles, especially those with some visible roots, such as windswept, root-over-rock, and rock-clasping styles.

SPECIAL FEATURES: *C. betulus* and *C. caroliniana* have muscled gray bark; fall color ranges from yellow-green to orange, red and yellow, depending upon the species.

HARDINESS: *C. betulus*, Zone 5; *C. caroliniana*, Zone 3; *C. coreana*, Zone 6; *C. laxiflora* (loose-flowered hornbeam), Zone 6; *C. japonica* (Japanese hornbeam), Zone 5; *C. turczaninovii*, Zone 5.

LIGHT: Partial shade, especially in midsummer, to full sun.

SOIL: Moist, well-drained soil; standard bonsai mix.

WATER: Not drought-tolerant. Keep soil from drying out.

FERTILIZER: Every two weeks during the growing season. After repotting, avoid feeding for two months.

PRUNING: This vigorous tree needs severe pruning. Cut back new shoots from five or six leaves to the first two leaves on the stem.

REPOT: Every one to two years for young trees before buds open in spring; every two to three years for older trees that grow less vigorously. When root pruning, cut off taproots below the tree base and half of the overall root mass.

PESTS AND DISEASES: Usually healthy; some leaf spot, powdery mildew, canker, spider mites, leaf miner, and dieback.

STYLES: Curved-trunk; straight-trunk; root-over-rock, windswept, and other styles with exposed roots.

CULTIVARS: *C. betulus* 'Incisa' has smaller leaves than the species.

The curved, tapered trunk of *C. betulus* rises from a muscled base.

Celtis occidentalis
SEL-tis ahk-si-den-TAL-iss

HACKBERRY
Ulmaceae

Native to eastern North America and the Midwest, hackberry may reach more than 60 feet high and tolerates drought, pollution, wind, and most soil types. Its deciduous leaves grow up to 5 inches long, and its sweet edible fruit turns from red or yellow to purple and measures about ¼ inch in diameter. This hardy spreading tree from the elm family makes a good bonsai candidate because the leaf size and spaces between nodes shrink drastically with bonsai pruning. When pruned for bonsai, the secondary branches

and twigs droop, giving the tree a graceful appearance.

SPECIAL FEATURES: ½ inch wide, edible red or yellow fruits that turn to purple.

HARDINESS: Zone 3. Needs winter protection below 15° F.

LIGHT: Full sun, but tolerates sun and partial shade in the South.

SOIL: Prefers rich, moist soil but tolerates just about anything. Plant in standard bonsai mix.

WATER: Water this tree frequently during the growing season. Give less water in winter.

FERTILIZER: Feed hackberry every month from spring to fall with a balanced liquid fertilizer.

PRUNING: Trim shoots back from four buds to two during the growing season. Cut back branches before growth begins in spring.

REPOT: Every two to four years in early spring in a deep bonsai dish, depending upon the age of the tree and its root development.

PESTS AND DISEASES: Free of Dutch elm disease but sometimes troubled by leaf spot, mites, scales, galls, and witches' brooms.

STYLES: Most styles except broom.

CULTIVARS AND SPECIES: *C. sinensis*, Japanese hackberry: up to 40 feet high, dark-green glossy leaves, ½-inch orange to red-brown fruits. Zone 7.

Proper pruning shrinks the size of long hackberry leaves and diminishes the length of the internodes.

C. sinensis, Japanese hackberry, has a naturally spreading form.

Celtis formosana, Formosan hackberry, has an air of refinement.

Chaenomeles
Kee-NAH-muh-leez

FLOWERING QUINCE
Rosaceae

This tough thorny shrub—grown in the garden for its flowers, its fragrant fruit, and as a barrier hedge—is a traditional bonsai plant. Before leafing out in spring, it produces lovely single (five-petal flowers) or double (more than five petals) blooms tinted pink, red, cream, white, salmon, or orange. In autumn, this deciduous shrub bears fragrant yellowish fruit flushed with some red. Although tart, this fruit is edible and used for jelly making. In winter, flowering quince looks coarse and stiff because of its gnarled, spiny stems. Although reddish when unfurling, the leaves of flowering quince mature to a deep, shiny green with no fall color. Many flower colors and cultivars exist.

SPECIAL FEATURES: Flowers of red, pink, cream, white, salmon, and orange appear in early spring before leaves. Sweetly scented fruit arrives in the fall.

HARDINESS: Zone 4.

LIGHT: Full sun to partial shade. Plant in full sun for maximum bloom and fruit set.

SOIL: Adaptable, but prefers soils with neutral to slightly low pH. Use regular bonsai mix.

WATER: During the growing period, needs daily watering. Keep water from splashing flowers and fruit. In winter, *Chaenomeles* requires just enough water to prevent dehydration during dormancy.

FERTILIZER: After blooming, feed soluble fertilizer every two weeks until leaf drop.

PRUNING: Cut off withered blooms unless you want the plant to set fruit. In autumn, prune new growth to two nodes and eliminate suckers unless necessary for styling.

REPOT: Every two years in the fall.

PESTS AND DISEASES: Leaf spot, mites, scale, and aphids. Overall this plant is a survivor.

STYLES: Because of its gnarly, twiggy suckering habit, flowering quince works especially well in styles with multiple stems, such as clump, five-trunk, cascade, semi-cascade, root-linked, raised-root, and raft styles. Its growth is too irregular for broom or straight-trunk styles.

CULTIVARS AND SPECIES:
C. japonica, Japanese flowering quince: popular bonsai species with red to orange flowers.

'Chojubai', a dwarf form with little red flowers.

'Chojubai White', a dwarf variety with light yellow flowers.

C. speciosa, common flowering quince, vigorous suckering shrub; 'Contorta' has twisted stems and foliage, available with white, red, or salmon pink blooms; 'Nivalis' produces clean white flowers.

C. 'Texas Scarlet': Lavish red blooms on a short suckering plant.

C. 'Toyo Nishiki': This curious and desirable cultivar turns out pink, white, and red flowers on the same plant and sometimes on the same thorny branch. Often, pink and white flowers appear together and red blooms are on another branch that either occurs naturally on the shrub or is a graft. Some susceptibility to fire blight.

C. japonica in the twin-trunk style has a stiff yet graceful habit with sparse flowers and tangled, exposed roots.

Chamaecyparis
Kam-ee-SIP-uh-ris

FALSE CYPRESS
Cupressaceae

These evergreen conifers originate in Asia and North America. Grow them outdoors in bonsai containers, giving them protection from winter wind and frost. Although the typical false cypress produces dark green leaves, cultivars are available in hues ranging from blue-green to golden yellow and chartreuse. The texture of false cypress varies. *C. pisifera* 'Filifera', for example, bears threadlike shoots covered with deep green scalelike leaves, giving it a fine texture. *C. obtusa*, on the other hand, looks coarser because its flattish fans of dense, overlapping foliage create dramatic contrasts of light and dark on the plant's surface.

SPECIAL FEATURES: Evergreen conifer with diverse, multihued cultivars, including many dwarfs.

HARDINESS: *C. lawsoniana* and *C. obtusa*, Zone 5; *C. nootkatensis*, *C. pisifera*, *C. thyoides*, Zone 4.

LIGHT: Full sun. If false cypress receives inadequate light, the inner and lower branches will die.

SOIL: To avoid root rot, plant in fast-draining bonsai mix.

WATER: Water early in the day, regularly during the growing season, letting soil dry slightly before each watering.

The reddish peeling bark and evergreen leaves of *C. pisifera* 'Tsukumo', Sawara false cypress, show to advantage in this twin-trunk style bonsai.

FERTILIZER: Feed with water-soluble fertilizer every two weeks from early spring to the middle of autumn.

PRUNING: Pinch tips of young shoots to shape the tree throughout the growing season. Scissor pruning will turn trimmed leaves brown. Also, avoid pruning back to old wood because the tree needs new wood to bud.

REPOT: Every two to four years for young trees, three to five years for older trees.

PESTS AND DISEASES: Root rot, needle and twig blights, spruce mites, scale.

STYLES: Most styles, including straight-trunk, curved-trunk, slanted, windswept, and literati. Do not use *Chamaecyparis* for the broom style, which looks better on upright deciduous trees with slender stems.

CULTIVARS AND SPECIES: *C. pisifera* 'Plumosa Compressa', dwarf plume false cypress looks more open and airy than *C. pisifera*, Sawara false cypress. Leaves are dark green on top with a pattern of silver marks below, and bark is an attractive ruddy brown.

C. nootkatensis, Nootka false cypress—even nonweeping forms droop. Dark green, scaly mature leaves hang in long, shaggy sprays off branches. Bark, arranged in vertical peeling strips on mature trees, ages to handsome silver-gray.

C. obtusa 'Nana Gracilis', dwarf Hinoki false cypress, has dark green leaf fans, a densely branched habit, and reddish brown bark. *C. obtusa* 'Nana Aurea' is a shrub with golden leaves that turn greenish when grown in some shade.

C. pisifera 'Plumosa Compressa', dwarf plume false cypress, is notable for its delicate form.

Cotoneaster
Koh-TOH-nee-ass-ter

COTONEASTER
Rosaceae

Cotoneaster is so easily cultivated and tolerant of human error that both beginning and advanced bonsai growers like working with it. This shrub, native to China and the Himalayas, has small glossy leaves, red fruits, and pink or white flowers.

A glazed blue pot enhances red fruits.

A weeping style suits this *C. horizontalis* bonsai.

Often used in the landscape for groundcover, several species also make good bonsai plants to grow outdoors. Cotoneaster's appealing attributes include a tight arching habit with intricate branching, diminutive leaves, pretty flowers, and decorative fruits. Cotoneaster can be evergreen, deciduous, or both, depending on the climate where it grows. It tends to root where it touches ground.

SPECIAL FEATURES: Pink or white flowers in spring, outstanding red, orange or yellow berries in fall; evergreen in moderate climates, deciduous in cold climates.

HARDINESS: Zone 4, 5, 6, or 7, depending on species. All need winter protection when grown as bonsai trees.

LIGHT: Full sun to partial shade.

SOIL: Well-drained soil. Plant in fast-draining bonsai mix.

WATER: Water daily or as necessary in summer. In winter, water just enough to avoid dehydration.

FERTILIZER: Every two weeks with soluble fertilizer except when flowering and fruiting.

PRUNING: Cut back old stems in early spring before new growth begins and new shoots to one or two nodes throughout the growing season. Encourage trunk growth by cutting down suckers at the base. Cotoneaster tolerates severe pruning. Wire stems in early spring before buds break.

REPOT: Every one to two years in spring. Prune off up to one third of root system.

PESTS AND DISEASES: Leaf blight, fireblight, mites, aphids, scale.

STYLES: Train cotoneaster into any of many styles, including semi-cascade, cascade, *mame*, clump, root-over-rock, sinuous, and curved-trunk styles.

CULTIVARS AND SPECIES:

C. adpressus, creeping cotoneaster, pink flowers, bright red fruits, prostrate dwarf deciduous shrub; undulating, glossy dark green leaves, red fall color; Zone 4b. 'Tom Thumb', also known as 'Little Gem', forms a 4- to 8-inch spreading mound of shiny tiny leaves on long stems.

C. apiculatus, cranberry cotoneaster, deciduous prostrate shrub with shiny green leaves, undulating margins, and red to reddish purple fall color; white flowers flushed red; round red fruits. Zone 4.

C. congestus, Pyrenees cotoneaster, miniature evergreen shrub shaped like a haystack with dull bluish-green leaves, white flowers tinged pink, red fruits, good for *mame*. Slow-growing Himalayan 'Likiang' has arched stems, pink flowers, red fruits; Zone 6.

C. dammeri, bearberry cotoneaster, prostrate evergreen to semi-evergreen shrub with leaves that are glossy and dark in summer and fall and dull green flushed with purple in winter; white flowers, scanty bright red fruit; 'Royal Beauty' has abundant coral red fruit; Zone 5.

C. horizontalis, rockspray cotoneaster, densely layered mound of flat, fishbonelike branches, pink flowers followed by shiny red fruits in late summer to fall.

C. microphyllus 'Cooperi', littleleaf cotoneaster, dwarf shrub with white flowers, vivid red fruits, miniature leaves that are shiny dark green on top, fuzzy gray below. 'Thymifolius', thyme-leaf cotoneaster, has tiny narrow leaves with edges that turn under covering stiff branches; Zone 5.

Crassula ovata
(also known as *C. argentea*)
KRASS-yew-luh oh-VAY-tuh

JADE PLANT
Crassulaceae

This South African native, grown for its round-tipped succulent leaves and chunky stems, is easy to propagate and to train into a bonsai tree. In the landscape, this upright branching shrub can grow 6 feet tall and 3 feet wide. Star-shaped blooms in light pink or white appear in spring. Jade plant can survive periods of parched soil, glaring sun, and extreme heat.

SPECIAL FEATURES: Fat, juicy yellowish green leaves, often edged in red; turgid stems; clusters of white to light pink flowers in spring. Very easy to grow.

HARDINESS: Zone 8b. Grow indoors in sunny window year-round. In summer, grow lightly shaded plants outdoors when temperatures are warmer than 50° F. May experience some leaf drop with changes in location or seasonal lighting.

LIGHT: Full sun.

SOIL: Well drained with neutral pH. Plant in regular bonsai mix.

WATER: Water jade plant thoroughly but carefully during the growing season, letting the soil dry out before each watering; water it infrequently in winter.

FERTILIZER: Feed with balanced liquid fertilizer monthly during the growing season.

PRUNING: Snip or pinch terminal buds when new growth is about 1 inch high. Difficult to wire.

REPOT: Any time, except periods of vigorous growth. Every one to two years for young trees under 10 years old; three to five years for older trees. Avoid root pruning as much as possible since it can weaken the plant. Wait one to two weeks before watering after repotting to avoid problems with root rot.

PESTS AND DISEASES: Mealybugs, aphids, root rot.

STYLES: Curved-trunk, twin-trunk, triple-trunk, clump.

CULTIVARS AND SPECIES: *C. ovata* 'Bronze Beauty', slow growing with little copper-tinged green leaves. *C. ovata* 'Sunset', gold-edged leaves in bright light.

C. sarcocaulis, grayish leaves; pink summer flowers; grow in light shade.

This *C. ovata* bonsai in the curved-trunk style has a thick trunk and limbs. In bright light, foliage may have red margins.

Crataegus
Krah-TEE-gus

HAWTHORN
Rosaceae

These thorny deciduous trees make appealing bonsai plants to grow outdoors. The best have four seasons of interest: May-blooming flowers in white, pink, or red; glossy green leaves turning red in the fall; shiny red fruits, known as haws, in autumn; and exfoliating bark for winter interest. In the landscape, hawthorns are small rounded trees with crowded thorny branches emerging low on the trunk. The challenges with these plants come from handling the spine-covered branches and from pest and disease problems that occur on some hawthorn species.

SPECIAL FEATURES: Profuse flower clusters in pink, white, or red; small, lustrous green leaves; red fall color on some species; glossy red fruits attractive to wildlife; peeling bark.

HARDINESS: Zone 4 or 5, depending on the species; all varieties require winter protection.
LIGHT: Full sun to partial shade.
SOIL: Tolerant of many soils. Standard bonsai mix.
WATER: During the growing season, water daily or as necessary but do not waterlog the soil. In winter, water less often. Never let hawthorn's soil grow parched.

C. cuneata, Japanese hawthorn, produces white blooms followed by large, bright red berries in fall.

Depending upon the variety, a hawthorn produces flowers ranging in color from white to bright red.

FERTILIZER: Every two weeks with liquid fertilizer when tree is in active growth.

PRUNING: Trim new growth in summer. If necessary, repeat on new stems in the fall. When possible, use cutting-grown material on its own roots instead of grafts since the root base of grafted plants can sucker prolifically after pruning, creating a maintenance hassle.

REPOT: Repot in early spring. Do plants up to 10 years old every one to two years; repot older plants every three to five years.

PESTS AND DISEASES: Rusts, mildews, leaf blight, aphids, scales, and caterpillars.

STYLES: Curved-trunk, slanted, windswept, literati, root-over-rock, all multitrunk styles

CULTIVARS AND SPECIES:

C. monogyna, singleseed (common) hawthorn, fragrant white flower clusters; dark red haws; Zone 4.

C. cuneata, Japanese hawthorn, single white blooms, yellow fall color, primarily grown for its dramatic 1-inch fruits; Zone 5.

C. laevigata 'Crimson Cloud', English hawthorn; clustered single red flowers with white star in the middle, shiny red fruits, dark green leaves, little to no fall color, resistant to leaf blight; 'Paul's Scarlet', showy, deep pink double flowers, prone to leaf blight; Zone 5.

C. viridis 'Winter King', Winter King green hawthorn; native to the Southeast and Midwest with four seasons of interest—exfoliating bark; glossy green leaves; abundant white flowers in late spring; outstanding scarlet red fruits on tree from summer to late winter; red fall color. Less prone to rust than many hawthorns. Takes moisture, Zone 4.

C. phaenopyrum, Washington hawthorn, abundant clusters of white flowers, glossy green leaves turning orange and red in fall, shiny red fruit adorn this native of the Southeast.

Cryptomeria japonica
Krip-toh-MAY-ree-uh jah-PON-y-kuh

JAPANESE CEDAR
Taxodiaceae

In ideal conditions, Japanese cedar grows up to 100 feet tall. Its tall stature, ornamental red-brown peeling bark, and tight evergreen foliage give it a noble habit. The leaves look like tiny dark green to bluish green spikes. Grow this evergreen bonsai outdoors but provide winter protection from wind and frost.

SPECIAL FEATURES: Flaky reddish bark, evergreen foliage tinged bronze in winter, attractive conical pattern of growth.

HARDINESS: Zone 6. Japanese cedar needs winter protection.

LIGHT: Full sun to light shade. Shade the tree from strong winds and harsh summer sun, which can dehydrate the needles and turn them brown.

SOIL: In nature, needs moist, acid, well-drained soil. Plant in standard bonsai mix.

WATER: Daily during the growing season. Likes humid sites, so mist leaves at least once a day in warm weather. Less water in winter, but keep soil from drying out.

FERTILIZER: Every two weeks during active growth.

PRUNING: To promote bushy growth, hand pinch growing tips frequently throughout the growing season. Scissoring turns tips brown. Remove growth near the trunk and on the underside of branches to circulate air and to expose handsome bark and trunk shape. You can broaden selected branches by letting them grow before styling. Wire in late spring.

REPOT: Every two to five years, depending on the age and vigor of the tree, in mid- to late spring.

PESTS AND DISEASES: Scale, red spider mites, tip and branch dieback.

STYLES: Straight-trunk, twin-trunk, sinuous, raft, group, rock-growing and tray-planting styles.

CULTIVARS: 'Elegans Nana', slow growing to 6 feet; rounded, bushy mound of blue-green needled branches.

'Globosa Nana', 4- to 8-foot, compact, blue-green hemisphere.

'Lobbii', smaller than species (up to 40 feet high), erect conical shape, disease resistant.

'Lobbii Nana', 4-foot dwarf with profuse dark green foliage.

This *C. japonica*, Japanese cedar, has one dominant and several lesser trunks.

Fagus
FAY-gus

BEECH
Fagaceae

Beeches look tall and majestic in the landscape, sometimes reaching 120 feet high. When planted singly in a sunny open space, they have vast spreading canopies thick with branches; planted more closely in groups, they have an oval habit. From fall to spring, tan leaves cling to the branches, shielding new buds and adding to the tree's seasonal interest. This deciduous tree is an excellent bonsai to grow outdoors not only for its beauty but also for its tolerance of drastic pruning.

SPECIAL FEATURES: Smooth gray bark; persistent, wavy oval leaves; gleaming, brown pointed buds like rolled cigars.

HARDINESS: Zone 4; needs winter protection when treated as bonsai.

LIGHT: Full sun to partial shade. Beech is vulnerable to leaf scorch so keep trees lightly shaded from summer sun.

SOIL: Moist, acid, well drained; standard bonsai mix.

WATER: Every day in the growing season. Keep leaves dry when watering to avoid leaf scorch. Water beeches less in winter, but never let the soil dry out.

FERTILIZER: After buds open, wait a month to start fertilizing. Then feed every two weeks until summer's end.

PRUNING: Pinch shoots back to two nodes in early summer. Shape by pruning when possible. If necessary, wire branches in midsummer but remove wires carefully after a few months. During active growth, remove some but never all leaves to reduce their size. Avoid leaf pruning after repotting.

REPOT: In spring before leaves open; every two to five years, depending upon the age and root development of the tree.

PESTS AND DISEASES: Usually healthy, but fungi can invade trees damaged by leaf scorch, making the tree susceptible to borers and scales.

STYLES: Curved, straight, twin-trunk, triple-trunk, clump, raft, group.

CULTIVARS AND SPECIES:
F. grandifolia, American beech, native to eastern North America, with smooth silvery gray bark, wide spreading branches, and vigorous suckering growth.

F. sylvatica, European beech, oval crown, low branches, formal, available with leaf colors ranging from variegated green and white or yellow to purple, copper, and variegated red, pink, and white.

■ 'Rohanii', purple-brown foliage, strong upright growth.

■ 'Asplenifolia', ferny leaves with gold-brown fall color.

■ 'Rotundifolia', shiny dark rounded foliage that is smaller than species with short leaf internodes.

F. crenata, Japanese white-barked beech, shorter, thinner trunk and smaller leaf size than previous species; light bark accentuated by bleaching nearly white with lime-sulphur. Good for group planting.

Beech trees take radical pruning, making them good bonsai subjects.

European beech's smooth, clean gray bark adds to the beauty of bonsai in the straight-trunk style.

Japanese white-barked beech in the curved-trunk style holds dead leaves through winter.

Ficus microcarpa (syn. *retusa*)
FY-kus my-kroh-KAR-pah

FIG, INDIAN LAUREL, BANYAN
Moraceae

This tropical plant from Southeast Asia makes an effective, low-maintenance bonsai. Its small glossy evergreen leaves, substantial trunk, exposed aerial roots, and gray to ruddy-gray bark look attractive all year. Figs can grow indoors year-round in warm climates or live outside in the summer. Some figs may develop aerial roots that thicken and grow when the tips stretch down into the soil. Figs forgive the blunders of beginning bonsai growers. If you forget to water them for a few days, they will probably survive.

SPECIAL FEATURES: Shiny evergreen leaves; easy to grow.

HARDINESS: Grow outdoors when nighttime temperatures are above 60° F. Avoid windy outdoor sites and drafty indoor locations.

LIGHT: Keep near a bright window or under grow-lights indoors; outdoors grow in full sun, filtered sun, or partial shade.

SOIL: Moist, well-drained soil. Standard bonsai mix.

WATER: Water daily or every other day and mist leaves frequently during the growing season. Wait until the soil dries out before watering in winter. Figs can survive some drought, but overwatering causes root rot and may kill them. Indoors, set the bonsai dish on a humidity tray filled with damp pebbles.

FERTILIZER: Monthly with a liquid food.

With age, a *F. philippinensis* bonsai in the clump style will develop a complicated pattern of stems and basal and aerial roots.

PRUNING: Leaf prune in spring or preferably at the end of summer. Prune shoots to two or three nodes to control growth. Style by wiring or pruning. Defoliate in summer to reduce leaf size.

REPOT: Every two years in spring.

PESTS AND DISEASES: Scales, mealybugs, spider mites, leaf spots, and dieback.

STYLES: Most styles, especially clump and other multitrunk styles, group, raised-root, raft, broom, root-over-rock.

CULTIVARS AND SPECIES: *F. benjamina*, weeping fig, including

F. benjamina, 'Too Little', 10-inch dwarf with diminutive leaves and trim growth.

F. benjamina, 'Variegata', shiny green and white leaves.

F. neriifolia, willow-leaved fig, bright green, narrow leaves resembling willow.

The broom style shows off the thick gnarly trunk and spreading proportions of this banyan, *F. microcarpa* 'Retusa'.

F. benjamina is easy for beginners to grow and with care trains into a handsome bonsai.

Gardenia augusta 'Radicans'
Gar-DEE-nee-uh aw-GUS-tuh
ra-di-KANZ

DWARF GARDENIA, DWARF CAPE JASMINE
Rubiaceae

From about May to July, dwarf gardenia bears petite 1- to 2-inch double white blooms exuding a strong, sweet perfume. As the flowers age, their thick petals change from white to creamy yellow. Everything about this shrub is small, from its 2×4-foot size to its glossy, dark green, leathery leaves. You can grow this broadleaf evergreen outdoors as long as the temperature stays above 35°F. If you live in a cool climate, bring the gardenia into a garage, shed, or basement until warm temperatures return.

SPECIAL FEATURES: Powerfully fragrant white flowers.

HARDINESS: Zone 8, with protection from frost and wind.

LIGHT: Full sun to partial shade.

SOIL: Moist, well-drained, acid soil high in organic matter. Plant in acid bonsai mix.

WATER: At least once a day from early spring to fall. Water less frequently in winter, but never let the soil dry out.

FERTILIZER: When plant is not flowering, feed twice a month from spring to fall, using a product for acid-loving plants.

PRUNING: To create a network of branches, prune new shoots from five leaves to two or three. Cut back big branches after blooming. Wire woody stems from late spring to fall without harming the tender bark.

REPOT: Every year or two. Severe root pruning can harm gardenias' fragile surface roots. It is better to repot frequently, trimming a small number of roots with each repotting.

PESTS AND DISEASES: Whiteflies, aphids, scales, powdery mildew, canker, bacterial leaf spot.

STYLES: Most styles, especially curved-trunk and multitrunk styles. The gardenia's dense shrubby habit does not suit broom, literati, or straight-trunk styles.

Shiny evergreen leaves and intensely fragrant flowers from May to July make *G. augusta* 'Radicans' a memorable bonsai, whether you grow it indoors or outdoors.

Ginkgo biloba
GING-koh by-LOH-bah

MAIDENHAIR TREE, GINKGO
Ginkgoaceae

Grown for its brilliant yellow fall color and unusual fan-shaped leaves, slow-growing ginkgo matures into a stately, erect tree that is sometimes wider than tall. Columnar to conical in youth, ginkgo thrives almost anywhere and is pest and disease resistant. It tolerates cold, heat, humidity, polluted air, and many soil types. Thus, ginkgo is an excellent choice for a medium to large deciduous bonsai outdoors. Ginkgo has male and female plants but buy males when possible. The edible fruits of old females have an unpleasant odor. Millions of years ago, this ancient tree was native to North America but disappeared until it was reintroduced in the 18th century from China.

SPECIAL FEATURES: Fan-shaped, light green leaves, bright yellow fall color.

HARDINESS: Zone 4, with winter protection, especially for roots.

LIGHT: Full sun to partial shade.

SOIL: In nature, it grows in most conditions, including acid and alkaline soils. Plant in standard bonsai mix.

WATER: From spring to fall, water every day. In winter, keep ginkgo's turgid roots well protected and almost dry so they do not rupture in cold weather.

PRUNING: Prune shoots on young trees to four or five nodes and on older trees to one or two nodes in early spring and midfall. Prune branches before new growth begins. Avoid wiring or first wrap the branch with raffia since ginkgo has fragile bark. If you wire, inspect the tree regularly to make sure the wire has not grown too tight.

FERTILIZER: Every two weeks with liquid fertilizer from spring to fall.

REPOT: Every one to five years, depending upon the age of the plant, in spring before new growth begins. When young, prune fleshy roots lightly.

PESTS AND DISEASES: Healthy under most conditions.

STYLES: Broom, straight-trunk, curved-trunk, clump, and other styles that accentuate ginkgo's natural upright habit.

CULTIVARS: 'Princeton Sentry', upright male form with slight taper from apex to base.

'Autumn Gold', broad symmetrical male with outstanding fall color.

Maidenhair tree in the group style looks like a miniature grove with dominant and secondary trunks encircled by lesser trunks.

Hedera helix
HED-ur-ah HEE-liks

ENGLISH IVY
Araliaceae

This woody vine, which can climb almost 100 feet up a tree, also makes a versatile bonsai with dark evergreen leaves and a ridged trunk. The handsome foliage, usually glossy and somewhat leathery, varies according to its age. Young leaves are very dark green with contrasting light veins. Old leaves are lighter green and have less prominent veins. Because ivy tolerates low-light conditions, it can grow indoors or outdoors.

SPECIAL FEATURES: Familiar shiny lobed evergreen leaves with white or light veins.

HARDINESS: Zone 4 with winter protection, depending upon the cultivar. Can also grow indoors.

LIGHT: Partial shade is best for bonsai. In nature English ivy can thrive in full sun or deep shade, though leaves may show some damage in strong sunlight.

SOIL: Fertile, well-drained soil high in organic matter. Use standard bonsai mix.

WATER: Daily throughout the growing season.

FERTILIZER: Every two weeks from spring to fall with liquid fertilizer.

PRUNING: Cut new shoots back to one or two leaves. Ivy tolerates severe pruning.

REPOT: Every two years in early spring or as needed.

PESTS AND DISEASES: Mites, aphids, mealybugs, and leaf spot.

STYLES: Root-over-rock, raised-root, slanted, clump, cascade, semi-cascade, and most other styles except for straight-trunk.

CULTIVARS: 'Plume d'Or', skinny little leaves and chartreuse stems on dense shrubby dwarf (Zone 7).

'Shamrock', small overlapping, deep green foliage on branching stems (Zone 7).

'Tres Coupé', dense little bush with short jointed stems (Zone 7).

'Spetchley' ('Gnome' or 'Minima'), tiny blackish green foliage tinged purple in winter on the smallest of all ivies (Zone 7).

'Telecurl' ('Little Picture'), small form with curly leaves and corkscrew stems; excellent for training into a coiled trunk (Zone 8).

The adventitious roots and vigorous trailing nature of ivy make it well suited to dramatic styles such as rock-growing and root-over-rock styles.

Ilex crenata 'Green Dragon'
I-leks kreh-NAH-tah

DWARF JAPANESE HOLLY
Aquifoliaceae

In the garden, *Ilex crenata* 'Green Dragon' stands 2 feet tall and wide. Its small size, fine texture, and asymmetrical shape give it a sculptured appearance. Shiny dark green miniature leaves about ¼ inch high and wide pack branches with short internodes. Even without pruning, this slow-growing evergreen looks like a bonsai. It reproduces sexually with distinct male and female forms. 'Dwarf Pagoda', the female counterpart to 'Green Dragon', produces tiny persistent fruits under the leaves. Grow this holly outdoors in a sheltered spot with adequate winter protection if you live in Zone 6 or higher.

SPECIAL FEATURES: Glossy, small foliage; short internodes; interesting irregular habit.

HARDINESS: Zone 6 with winter protection. In winter, shield leaves from dehydrating winds.

LIGHT: Full sun to light shade.

SOIL: Light, somewhat acid soil. Plant in standard bonsai mix.

WATER: Daily during the growing season. Protect roots from deep frost, and water when dry.

FERTILIZER: Every two weeks from spring to fall.

PRUNING: Because *I. crenata* has fragile stems, shape it by pruning instead of wiring if possible, eliminating excess branches and trimming shoots to two or three nodes after new growth hardens.

REPOT: Every two years in spring.

PESTS AND DISEASES: Spider mites, aphids, scales; foliage may yellow in very alkaline soils.

STYLES: Most styles except straight-trunk and broom.

CULTIVARS: 'Dwarf Pagoda', almost identical to 'Green Dragon' but with shiny, black berry-like fruit.

'Stokes', male with dense dome-like shape, hardy to Zone 5.

With its fine texture and tiny evergreen leaves, dwarf Japanese holly is well-suited to training as a small bonsai.

Jasminum nudiflorum
Jaz-MEE-num nu-dee-FLOH-rum

WINTER JASMINE
Oleaceae

The long, light green trailing branches of winter jasmine add a splash of bright color to the winter palette. Its profuse square stems form a spreading mound that is striking when it tumbles over walls. Only the young stems are green. The brown, woody older branches create a neutral backdrop that intensifies the green of the newer stems. In the depths of winter from January to March, the bare stems produce dark reddish buds that unfold into bright yellow blooms. Flowers are slender ½- to ¾-inch tubes opening into six flat, rounded, petallike segments. After blooming, dark glossy green leaves appear on the branches, which root where they touch the soil.

SPECIAL FEATURES: Deep purplish red, lustrous buds open to clear yellow flowers; square bright green stems form showy winter mound.

HARDINESS: Zone 6 with adequate winter protection.

LIGHT: Sun to shade. Place in sun for maximum blooms except in the heat of summer, when it will benefit from afternoon shade.

SOIL: In the landscape, grow in any soil. Plant in standard bonsai mix.

WATER: Daily in the growing season. Give it less water in winter, but do not let it dry out.

FERTILIZER: After blooming ceases in March, feed winter jasmine every two weeks until fall.

PRUNING: Trim shoots to the first pair of leaves. Trim branches after blooming in spring.

REPOT: Every other year in fall.

PESTS AND DISEASES: Scale, aphids, leaf spots.

STYLES: Most styles except straight-trunk, broom, literati.

CULTIVARS: 'Nanum', dwarf cultivar, grows slowly.

'Variegatum', gray-green centers edged in white; less robust than other species.

Valued for its early yellow blooms, winter jasmine, a woody vine, develops an old-looking, irregular trunk with persistent pruning.

Juniperus chinensis var. sargentii
Ju-NI-per-us chye-NEN-sis sar-JEN-tee-I

SARGENT JUNIPER
Cupressaceae

In its native Japan, this tough, hardy evergreen conifer lives on seacoasts and mountain crags. Sargent juniper grows no more than 2 feet tall but spreads up to 9 feet wide. Scalelike, blue-green leaves form fine-textured branchlets. The reddish brown bark peels off the tree in thin strips. Junipers produce male and female flowers and cones, sometimes on the same plant. Female cones look like dark blue or black ornamental berries. Because of its rugged character and tolerance for severe pruning, bonsai growers have trained Sargent juniper for centuries. It remains a popular hardy plant for bonsai use.

SPECIAL FEATURES: Shredding, reddish brown bark; bluish green, scalelike leaves that look like miniature branches.

HARDINESS: Zone 4 with sufficient winter protection.

LIGHT: Full sun.

SOIL: Tolerates most soils except wet ones. Plant juniper in extra-porous bonsai mix.

WATER: Daily from spring to fall.

FERTILIZER: Every two weeks with a liquid fertilizer throughout the growing season.

PRUNING: Takes well to pruning and wiring. During spring and summer, prune branches with bonsai shears and pinch fresh growth tips with fingers since shears cause cut leaves to go brown. Remove shoots and leaves from the bottoms and bases of branches so the styling of the trunk and main branches is apparent.

REPOT: In early spring every two years for trees up to 10 years old; every four to five years as needed for older juniper specimens.

PESTS AND DISEASES: Juniper blight, cedar-apple rust, red spider mites.

STYLES: Most styles except broom, which looks best on upright deciduous trees. Deadwood techniques enhance the aged appearance of Sargent juniper.

CULTIVARS: 'Viridis', stays clear green year-round.

Evergreen foliage pads at the branch tips keep the tapered trunk and branches of *J. chinensis* var. **sargentii** visible all year.

Juniperus procumbens 'Nana'
Ju-NI-per-us proh-KUM-benz NAH-nah

DWARF JAPANESE GARDEN JUNIPER
Cupressaceae

The branches of this dwarf juniper create a dense mound up to 2 feet high and 12 feet wide. Often grown as a sun-loving groundcover, the plant produces scaly mid-green foliage tinged purple in winter.

SPECIAL FEATURES: Low spreading habit; fine-textured leaves with a purplish tint in winter.

HARDINESS: Zone 4 with winter protection.

LIGHT: Full sun.

SOIL: Tolerates most soils. Thrives on difficult slopes with sharp drainage and high pH. Plant in fast-draining bonsai mix.

WATER: Daily during the growing season. Water less frequently in winter, but keep the soil from drying out.

FERTILIZER: Every two weeks with a liquid fertilizer throughout the growing season.

PRUNING: Takes well to pruning and wiring. During spring and summer, prune branches with bonsai shears and pinch fresh growth tips with fingers. Remove shoots and leaves from the bottoms and bases of branches so the styling of the trunk and main branches is apparent.

REPOT: In early spring every two years for trees up to 10 years old; every four to five years for older trees.

PESTS AND DISEASES: Juniper blight, cedar-apple rust, red spider mites.

STYLES: Its procumbent habit suits cascade and semi-cascade styles.

CULTIVARS AND SPECIES:
J. horizontalis, creeping juniper, is a groundcover fit for cascade and semi-cascade styles. Its leaves in shades of gray-green change to dark purple in winter.

The trunk of *J. procumbens* 'Nana' twists as it curves up toward the apex. Bleached *jins* and hollows (*sabamiki*) weather its appearance.

A deep octagonal pot and a simple pedestal in neutral hues stabilize the sweeping descent of this *J. horizontalis* cascade without detracting from the balanced form.

Juniperus rigida
Ju-NI-per-us RI-ji-duh

NEEDLE JUNIPER
Cupressaceae

In its natural habitat, *J. rigida* is a broad tree that grows up to 25 feet high and 20 feet wide with an open nature. This traditional bonsai tree develops branches that arc outward from the trunk and sag at the tips, giving it a graceful appearance. When trained for bonsai, however, it adapts to almost any style.

SPECIAL FEATURES: Sharp-needled foliage, shaggy brown bark; round blue-black fruits on the female.

HARDINESS: Zone 6 with winter protection.

LIGHT: Full sun.

SOIL: Tolerates most soils. Plant in fast-draining bonsai mix.

WATER: Daily during the growing season. Water junipers less frequently in winter, but keep the soil from drying out.

FERTILIZER: Every two weeks with a liquid fertilizer throughout the growing season.

PRUNING: Takes well to pruning and wiring. During spring and summer, prune branches with bonsai shears and pinch fresh growth tips with fingers. Remove shoots and leaves from the bottoms and bases of branches so the styling of the trunk and main branches is apparent.

REPOT: In early spring every two years for trees up to 10 years old; every four to five years as needed for older trees.

PESTS AND DISEASES: Juniper blight, cedar-apple rust, red spider mites.

STYLES: Shape this popular bonsai subject into any style except broom.

Jinning and *sharimiki* age this *J. rigida* bonsai in the informal-upright style.

Lagerstroemia indica
Lay-gur-STROH-mee-uh IN-di-kuh

COMMON OR CHINESE CRAPE MYRTLE
Lythraceae

Crape myrtle provides four seasons of interest to bonsai growers. The bark, smooth gray and peeling on the outside, sheds to reveal a mottled inner bark in some combination of brown, tan, russet, pink, cream, and gray. Removing low limbs exposes more of the trunk and makes the bark, which shows up best after leaf drop, more apparent. In addition to bark, the leaves turn red, yellow, and orange in autumn, often on the same tree. Many people, however, grow crape myrtle for its six-petaled red, white, pink, or purple flowers, which bloom from June or July through September, depending on the cultivar and the location.

SPECIAL FEATURES: Blossoms of white, pink, purple, or red; peeling multicolored bark; shiny dark green leaves that turn red, orange, or yellow in fall.

HARDINESS: Zone 7 with winter protection. Can also grow indoors in brightly lit location but needs cool temperatures (about 50° F) to trigger winter dormancy in the house.

LIGHT: Full sun.

SOIL: Moist, loamy, well-drained soil. Plant in standard bonsai mix.

WATER: Every day while in active growth. Examine frequently in winter, and water before the soil dries out.

FERTILIZER: Feed liquid fertilizer every two weeks from spring to fall.

PRUNING: Crape myrtle flowers at stem tips. After it blooms, cut shoots back to style and promote plentiful flowers the following year. When possible, shape by pruning since bark is fragile and wire can harm it.

REPOT: Every year or two in early spring before leaves unfurl.

PESTS AND DISEASES: Aphids; powdery mildew, particularly in spring and fall. Best to plant mildew-resistant varieties in full sun and give them good air circulation.

STYLES: Curved-trunk, slanted, clump, root-over-rock, cascade, and semi-cascade.

CULTIVARS: Look for National Arboretum hybrids, which are repeat bloomers and resist powdery mildew. Some dwarf or semi-dwarf multistemmed cultivars include:

'Chickasaw', 2×3-foot shrub, lavender blooms, bronzy red in fall.

'Tonto', 8 feet, deep red blossoms, maroon fall color.

'Apalachee', 12 feet, lavender flowers; orange, rust, and red in fall; mottled peeling cinnamon bark.

'Caddo', 8 feet, pink blooms, red-orange in fall, reddish peeling bark.

Reducing the foliage masses of this twin-trunk *L. indica* exposes its attractive multihued bark and branch structure.

Larix laricina
LAH-riks lah-ri-SEE-nuh

AMERICAN LARCH, TAMARACK
Pinaceae

Although some trees like hot weather, hardy tamarack, a deciduous conifer native to northern North America, does not. Tamarack grows about 10 feet tall at the Arctic Circle. Farther south, it can reach up to 75 feet. Its light green, needle-like leaves, occurring in bunches of 10 to 20, turn brilliant yellow before dropping in fall. The smooth young bark on the straight, thin larch trunk turns rough with age. Floppy needled twigs hang off its horizontal branches, giving the tree a pyramidal shape. Larch develops a wide, shallow root system. In nature, it appears near lakes or in bogs and swamps. Farther north, you can find it on drier sites. Fast growing when young, larch is an excellent choice for bonsai.

SPECIAL FEATURES: Needle-like, 1-inch

leaves with bright yellow fall color; female cones purplish in spring mature to brown.

HARDINESS: Zone 2 with winter protection below 15° F.

LIGHT: Full sun.

SOIL: Moist, preferably acid and boggy. Plant in standard bonsai mix.

WATER: At least once a day in the growing season, less in winter.

FERTILIZER: Every two weeks from April to September.

PRUNING: Pinch shoots to two bundles of needles until midsummer. Trim branches before growth begins.

REPOT: Every one to two years in early spring.

PESTS AND DISEASES: Sawfly, rust.

STYLES: Any style except broom.

CULTIVARS AND SPECIES: *L. decidua*, European larch, handsome tree that tolerates a bit more warmth; Zone 3.

Deadwood effects embellish the trunk and branches of a slanting-style larch.

Malus
MA-lus

CRABAPPLE
Rosaceae

Cultivated as bonsai for their ornamental buds, flowers, and fruits, crabapple trees differ from apple trees by the size of the fruit. Crabapples have fruit less than 2 inches across. Any *Malus* with bigger fruit is an apple tree. Hundreds of crabapple cultivars derive from about 25 species. In spring crabapples produce ornamental pink, red, or coral flower buds, followed by single or double, often sweetly scented, blossoms in white or tints of pink and rosy red. Attractive autumnal fruits vary from red to green, orange, and yellow. On some cultivars, fruits persist all winter.

The broad base and tapering rise of this crabapple trunk give it an air of steadfastness.

SPECIAL FEATURES: Rosy buds; white, pink, or rosy red, sometimes fragrant flowers; red, green, orange, or yellow fruit.

HARDINESS: Zone 4, depending on the variety, with winter protection.

LIGHT: Full sun for best fruiting.

SOIL: Moist, slightly acid, well-drained. Plant in standard bonsai mix.

WATER: At least once a day during the growing season, less in winter.

FERTILIZER: Start feeding soluble fertilizer every two weeks after flowers fade. Continue feeding to the end of summer.

PRUNING: Pinch fresh shoots back to two leaves after they flower. Cut overlong shoots back in fall. Prune suckers on grafted trees when they appear. For smaller leaves and internodes, you can do leaf cutting in spring.

REPOT: Every year in a deep container in spring or autumn.

PESTS AND DISEASES: Depending on the cultivar or species, susceptible to many pests and diseases, including aphids, Japanese beetles, cedar-apple rust, apple scab, and powdery mildew. Choose disease-resistant varieties of crabapple to avoid many of these problems.

STYLES: Most styles except broom, cascade, and formal upright.

CULTIVARS AND SPECIES:

M. 'Jewelberry', dense bushy tree with deep pink buds, fragrant white flowers, lustrous red fruits that last until January; 8×10 feet, Zone 5. Disease resistant.

M. sargentii, tough bushy tree, pink buds open to scented white blooms, dark red fruits through early winter, sometimes orangy fall color, 6×12 feet.

'Tina', deep pink buds open to white blossoms, small leaves, 4 to 6 feet high.

■ **The Round Table series:** These dwarfs are about half the standard crabapple size and bred for improved disease resistance. Some of the plants include:

Cinderella™, white flowers and tiny gold fruit; 8×5 feet.

King Arthur™, white flowers, clear red fruit, vigorous; 12×10 feet.

Crabapples produce colorful buds; pink or white frequently fragrant flowers; and red, gold, or orange fruits that sometimes last into winter.

Myrtus communis 'Compacta'
MEER-tus kom-MEW-nis kom-PAK-tuh

DWARF TRUE OR COMMON MYRTLE
Mytraceae

In a Mediterranean landscape, dwarf myrtle makes an attractive topiary or low hedge. This dense 4-foot Mediterranean shrub, a subtropical plant, has small shiny evergreen leaves redolent of spice when crushed. It has scented white flowers from spring to late summer, followed by blue-black fruits. Its tough, flexible stems and vigorous shoot production make it suitable for bonsai training. Using proper pruning and wiring, you can train it into a small bonsai tree. In cool climates, keep myrtle indoors in winter or year-round.

SPECIAL FEATURES: Perfumed white blooms, followed by deep-blue ½-inch berries; lustrous evergreen foliage, dense pattern of growth.

HARDINESS: Zone 9.

LIGHT: Full sun to partial shade. Grow indoors near a south or west window in winter. In summer set in bright, indirect light indoors or move outdoors after any danger of frost has passed. Keep well-ventilated indoors.

SOIL: Native to Mediterranean areas, it needs well-drained soil. Plant in free-draining bonsai mix.

WATER: Daily during the growing season when grown outdoors, less in winter. Soil should not dry out completely before watering. Indoors, check soil daily and water when almost dry.

FERTILIZER: Feed with a balanced fertilizer once per month during the growing season.

PRUNING: Pinch terminal buds when fresh shoots are about 1 inch long to promote side branching and the growth of thick leafy areas at the ends of branches. Prune or wire branches as needed for styling.

REPOT: Every one to five years, depending upon the tree's age and root vigor.

PESTS AND DISEASES: Scale, leaf spot, gray mold.

STYLES: Adapts to any style including curved-trunk, twin-trunk, clump, and group.

CULTIVARS: *M. c.* subspecies *tarentina*, 'Microphylla Variegata', tiny narrow leaves with creamy margins, pinkish blooms, and white berries.

Mytus communis 'Compacta' makes a versatile, easy-to-grow evergreen bonsai to grow indoors in cool climates.

Olea europaea
OH-lee-uh yu-ROH-pee-uh

OLIVE
Oleaceae

Olive trees, which can live for a thousand years, thrive in dry, gravely sites in areas with a Mediterranean climate, and in cool greenhouses. Tolerant to wind, drought, and salt, they produce leathery evergreen foliage that is shiny gray-green on top and silvery below. Scented blooms, edible fruits, and the cracked bark and jagged asymmetry of old trees make olive an interesting and unusual bonsai choice.

SPECIAL FEATURES: Fragrant creamy flower clusters in summer, edible fruits turning from green to black.

HARDINESS: Zone 9. Where not fully hardy, grow near a sunny sheltered wall to create a suitable microclimate in summer. Grow indoors in winter in very bright light. Grown outdoors, olive needs winter protection in a cool shed to keep roots and leaves from freezing.

LIGHT: Full sun.

SOIL: Need fast-draining bonsai mix with a high pH to simulate the rocky Mediterranean conditions that these trees favor.

WATER: Water with some restraint during the growing season and sparingly in winter.

FERTILIZER: Monthly feeding with balanced liquid fertilizer.

PRUNING: Pinch green stem tips and growth on underside of branches. Cut branches to shape in autumn. Rub out buds resulting from the cut, or you may see rough shoots crowd the area. Apply wire carefully when the tree is not in active growth or wrap branches with raffia before wiring since wire may damage the fragile bark of olive.

REPOT: Every two or three years in early spring before the leaves open.

Prune root mass and old foliage by one-third.

PESTS AND DISEASES: Scales, aphids, and spider mites.

STYLES: Curved-trunk, multi-trunk styles, and tray planting. Stay away from styles that uncover olive's tender roots.

Through bonsai training, olive develops an old-looking bark and tiny leaves. It can grow indoors year-round or outside when temperatures are warm.

Picea
Pye-SEE-ah

SPRUCE
Pinaceae

Hardy evergreen spruces originate in cool forested regions of the Northern Hemisphere. These undemanding conifers make excellent bonsai. Their leaves are needles that grow individually (not in bundles like pine foliage) around each stem. The bark adds to the tree's beauty, becoming scaly with age and ridged on the stock or lower trunk. Spruce roots are widespread and near the soil surface. Some bonsai artists take advantage of this feature by revealing sections of the surface roots, making the soil surface look gnarled and ancient. Spruce cultivars range from miniature globes for rock gardens to large icy blue or gold pyramidal trees.

SPECIAL FEATURES: Evergreen needled leaves, formal growth habit, hanging cones.

HARDINESS: Zone 2 or 3, depending on the species. Grow spruce outdoors, protecting the roots from deep frosts.

LIGHT: Full sun for landscape plants. Set bonsai in sun to partial shade.

SOIL: Neutral to acidic, moist, well-drained. Use standard bonsai mix.

WATER: Daily from spring to fall. Provide less water in winter, but never let the soil become totally dry.

FERTILIZER: Apply a balanced liquid feed every two weeks from spring to fall.

PRUNING: During the growing season, wait until shoots measure 1 inch before pinching them back by ¼ to ½ inch. Cut back branches and shape with wire in late autumn or winter. Some spruces are difficult to wire because they readily return to their former shape once the wire is removed. Rewiring may be needed.

P. glehnii, Sachalin spruce, (shown in the twin-trunk style) is a traditional bonsai subject in Japan.

REPOT: Every two years or as needed in spring before new growth begins or in the fall.

PESTS AND DISEASES: Aphids, mites, bagworms, rust.

STYLES: Except for broom, most styles including straight- and curved-trunk, windswept, and the full range of multitrunk styles. Deadwood details add age and personality to spruce bonsai.

CULTIVARS: *P. jezoensis* subspecies *hondoensis* (Yezo spruce), traditional species for Japanese bonsai. Yezo spruce grows up to 100 feet tall in nature with needles up to ¾ inch long.

P. glehnii (Sachalin spruce), traditional species for Japanese bonsai. Sachalin spruce produces shorter needles on a smaller tree.

P. glauca 'Conica', dwarf Alberta spruce, forms a 12-foot, tight shrubby cone.

P. abies 'Little Gem', Norway spruce, makes a dense green ball of tiny-needled, slow-growing stems.

The straight trunk is visible in this *P. glehnii,* Sachalin spruce, trained in the formal upright style.

P. glauca 'Echiniformis' is suitable for small bonsai because the cushion-shaped plant grows just 1 foot high in nature.

Pinus densiflora
PYE-nus den-si-FLOH-rab

JAPANESE RED PINE
Pinaceae

For hundreds of years people have transformed pine trees into bonsai. These hardy evergreen conifers produce needled leaves bundled in groups of two, three, or five. *P. densiflora* has shiny green needles bundled in twos. In the garden, *P. densiflora* can grow more than 40 feet high. Its open branches, level top, uneven shape, and bent or slanting trunk give it an eccentric charm. Japanese red pine makes an outstanding bonsai for growing outdoors in northern climates.

SPECIAL FEATURES: Japanese red pine has orange-red shredding bark furrowed and reddish-gray at the base of mature specimens; glossy clear green needles.

HARDINESS: Zone 3 with protection.

LIGHT: Full sun.

SOIL: Sandy soil that drains freely. Plant in fast-draining bonsai mix.

WATER: For the most part daily from spring to fall, checking first that the soil is fairly dry.

FERTILIZER: Every two weeks with liquid fertilizer during the growing season.

PRUNING: Prune by candling, or twisting off, emerging shoots before the needles develop in early summer. The more candles you remove, the more you restrict the growth of the tree. Take off larger branches in early spring or fall. Wire the tree when it is dormant.

REPOT: Every two to five years, depending on the age of the plant and the vigor of its roots.

PESTS AND DISEASES: Aphids, weevils, moths, mealybugs, sawfly, red pine scale, miners, borers, blights, root rot.

STYLES: Curved-trunk and multi-trunk styles particularly suit its informal habit.

CULTIVARS AND SPECIES: 'Alice Verkade' is a globular dwarf. 'Umbraculifera' is a 12-foot dwarf with rich orange bark.

P. mugo, Swiss mountain pine, has dark green needles in bundles of two. It is usually grown for its small varieties, including 'Mops', a 3×3-foot globe, and var. *pumilio*, which forms spreading 3×10-foot mounds.

The balanced asymmetry of the curved trunk style fits the irregular growth habit of Japanese red pine.

JAPANESE WHITE PINE
Pinaceae

Japanese white pine is a classic bonsai subject. This five-needled pine grows slowly to 50 feet tall in its natural setting, but in home landscapes it stands about half that size. Because of its abundant flexible branches and stiff leaves that occur in bunches at the stem tips, Japanese white pine lends itself to the formal-upright style. In maturity, *Pinus parviflora* loses its compact, conelike form and takes on a broader, more interesting shape.

SPECIAL FEATURES: Dark green needles with bluish white inner stripes; flaking brown bark; fine texture in the landscape.

HARDINESS: Zone 4.

LIGHT: Full sun. In hot climates, situate in light shade to avoid scorching leaves.

SOIL: Sandy soil that drains freely. Plant in fast-draining bonsai mix.

WATER: For the most part daily from spring to fall, checking first that the soil is fairly dry.

FERTILIZER: Apply balanced liquid fertilizer every two weeks during the growing season.

PRUNING: Prune by candling, or twisting off, emerging shoots before the needles develop in early summer. The more candles you remove, the more you restrict the growth of the tree. Take off larger branches in early spring or fall. Wire the tree when it is dormant.

REPOT: In early spring or early fall every two to five years, depending on the age of the plant and the vigor of its roots.

PESTS AND DISEASES: Miners, scales, borers, mealybugs, blight, rust, and root rot are widespread.

STYLES: This is the traditional plant for the straight-trunk style, but you can train *P. parviflora* in all styles except broom.

CULTIVARS: 'Adcock's Dwarf', at maturity a 3-foot ball with short bluish green needles bunched at the stem ends.

An interesting trunk base and handsome pads of foliage draw attention to Japanese white pine in the curved-trunk style.

Pinus thunbergii
PYE-nus thun-BAYR-gee-i

JAPANESE BLACK PINE
Pinaceae

Black pine originates on the windy crags of Japan's seacoast and is salt and wind tolerant. For centuries, bonsai growers have exaggerated its natural irregularity and its striking plated, furrowed bark. They give it an aged look by bending the branches down and thinning the packed twisted leaves, which grow in pairs. To enhance the tree's dramatic character and bring in sunlight, many bonsai makers pluck needles growing inside or under branches and near the trunk. This pruning creates subtle pads of fine-textured needles near the ends of branches and helps define the tree's silhouette. Pruning and shaping also expose the heavily fissured bark, probably this tree's greatest asset.

SPECIAL FEATURES: Rugged, gray-black bark with deep furrows; fine-textured, stiff, glossy needles.
HARDINESS: Zone 6 with adequate winter protection.
LIGHT: Full sun.
SOIL: Sandy soil that drains freely. Plant in fast-draining bonsai mix.

WATER: For the most part daily from spring to fall, checking first that the soil is fairly dry.
FERTILIZER: Every two weeks with liquid fertilizer throughout the growing season.
PRUNING: Prune by candling, or twisting off, emerging shoots before the needles develop. The more candle that you remove, the more you restrict the growth of the tree. Take off larger branches in early spring or fall, and wire the tree when dormant.
REPOT: Every two to five years, depending on the age of the plant and the vigor of its root system.

The dipped limbs and sinuous trunk of this Japanese black pine amplify its natural form.

PESTS AND DISEASES: Miners, scales, borers, blight, rust, and root rot are widespread.
STYLES: All styles except broom.
CULTIVARS: 'Koto Buki', a cone-shaped dwarf with small deep green needles and substantial stems.

'Yatsubusa', little needles, crowded growth, but otherwise similar to the species *P. thunbergii*.

Podocarpus macrophyllus
Poh-doh-KAR-puss mak-roh-FIL-us

CHINESE YEW, BIGLEAF PODOCARP, BUDDHIST PINE
Podocarpaceae

Grown for its glossy evergreen foliage, Chinese yew is a slow-growing, cone-shaped tree up to 50 feet tall. Reddish brown bark covers the upright trunk. The leaves, arranged in spirals, resemble dark green leathery spears 2 to 4 inches long. Podocarp, which thrives where the growing season is long, hot, and humid, has male and female plants. In fall, females produce edible red-purple fruit.

SPECIAL FEATURES: Shiny, needle-like evergreen leaves arranged in attractive spirals.

HARDINESS: Zone 8. In cooler areas, bring outdoors when temperatures are reliably warm.

LIGHT: Full sun to partial shade. For bonsai, a sunny area is best except in hot climates where afternoon sunlight may scorch needles.

SOIL: Rich, well-drained. Plant in standard bonsai mix.

WATER: Check daily and water when almost dry. Podocarp needs humidity indoors, so set the bonsai dish on a layer of moist pebbles on a flat humidity tray. Check pebbles for dampness daily and moisten them as needed.

FERTILIZER: Give balanced liquid fertilizer every two weeks during the growing season.

PRUNING: Trim branches before growth begins in spring. Pinch shoots by half when they begin opening to reduce needle size and maintain the shape.

REPOT: Every other year before growth begins in early spring.

PESTS AND DISEASES: Scale; wet soils and overwatering can cause root rot.

STYLES: Most styles except broom. *P. macrophyllus* is well-suited to straight-trunk style.

CULTIVARS AND SPECIES: 'Brodie', compact 3×6-foot shrub.

'Variegatus', green and white variegated leaves.

P. nivalis, alpine totara, slow-growing evergreen shrub up to 2 feet tall with 1-inch needles. Good plant for small-size bonsai; hardy with frost protection to Zone 7.

The styling of this Chinese yew draws attention to its evergreen leaves, set in spirals on the branches.

Prunus serrulata
PRU-nus sayr-yu-LAH-tah

JAPANESE FLOWERING CHERRY
Rosaceae

Grown for its prolific pink to white spring blooms and attractive leaves, Japanese flowering cherry is a bonsai classic. Blossoms vary from ½ to 2½ inches wide and may have five petals or more, depending on the cultivar. Changing leaf color provides additional interest. Red-flushed spring leaves mature to deep shiny green, and autumnal hues range from bronze to red. Japanese flowering cherry grows with vigor and can make a successful medium or large bonsai. Not all *Prunus* species (there are about 400 including cherry, apricot, plum, peach, and almond) make high-quality bonsai. Some bear edible stoned fruit; some produce short-lived showy flowers and fruits, and some have little value as cultivated plants. These deciduous trees grow outdoors with variable cold tolerance. As a genus, *Prunus* is susceptible to many pests and diseases of the rose family. If you want to train an ornamental cherry as a bonsai, consider choosing a variety resistant to pests and disease. When possible, select a tree grown on its own roots instead of a graft. Bad grafts may be the point of entry for pests and diseases and bulge as the tree matures. Regular maintenance helps keep your cherry tree healthy. Inspect your plant frequently and treat problems when small. In general, *Prunus* suffers dieback in cold climates, so use for bonsai in Zone 6 and higher. Birds eat the buds, so guard your bonsai.

SPECIAL FEATURES: Lavish pink blooms in spring; shiny black fruits, red-tinted glossy leaves in spring; bronze to red fall color.

HARDINESS: Zone 5 or 6 in the landscape, depending upon the cultivar. Grow cherry bonsai in Zone 6 and higher and give them winter frost protection.

LIGHT: Full sun.

SOIL: Most soils, especially when moist and well-drained. Plant in standard bonsai mix.

WATER: Daily during the growing season. Water less in winter, but do not let the soil dry out completely.

FERTILIZER: Every two weeks after the flowers have faded in the fall.

A teal rectangular pot ornaments the pink spring blossoms of this *Prunus* bonsai.

PRUNING: Cut back branches after flowering but before midsummer so that wounds heal quickly and diseases have less opportunity to infect the tree. Prune shoots to two buds after flowering. Wire the tree in summer.

REPOT: Every year after it flowers.

PESTS AND DISEASES: Aphids, scales, borers, canker, leaf spots, and fungal diseases.

STYLES: Any style except broom. Weeping varieties lend themselves to cascade and semi-cascade styles.

CULTIVARS: 'Snowgoose', white flowers, erect oval habit when young becomes spreading when older, to 20 feet, improved insect resistance.

P. 'Hally Jolivette', 15-foot shrub or small tree with delicate stems, pink buds open to double pale pink flowers that bloom up to 20 days, vigorous and pretty; Zone 5.

P. subhirtella 'Autumnalis', Higan cherry, fast-growing tree to 40 feet, handsome gray bark with pale horizontal marks known as lenticils, dark pink buds opening to pale pink 10-petal blooms fading to near-white, may have random fall bloom; fruits are oval red turning glossy black, tolerates cold and heat better than most cherries; Zone 4; 'Autumnalis Rosea' has pink flowers.

P. 'Okame', 20 to 30 feet high and wide, deep pink flowers bloom very early spring; bronze to scarlet fall color; ruddy brown bark with gray horizontal bands (lenticils) provide late fall and winter interest; excellent in warm climates; hardy to Zone 6.

P. mume, Japanese flowering apricot, grows about 25 feet high and wide with a rounded spreading canopy. Flowers on bare branches in late winter and early spring; this classic bonsai subject produces perfumed, 1-inch white to deep pink blooms, followed by round yellow edible fruits with a sour taste and a covering of tiny hairs. Hardy to Zone 6.

Deadwood on this elegant flowering apricot ages its twisted trunk.

Punica granatum 'Nana'
PU-ni-ka grah-NAY-tum NAH-nah

DWARF POMEGRANATE
Punicaceae

Pomegranates make excellent bonsai because of their arching habit and multiple stems. Trained as bonsai, these stems can develop into one or more broad, sometimes crooked trunks. These deciduous shrubs or small trees grow up to 20 feet high.

In spring, a copper tint colors the veins of the shiny narrow leaves. In summer, the plant bears scarlet flowers up to one and a half inches wide. The blooms appear individually at the branch tips or in clusters of up to five. Edible, round, yellow-brown or yellow-red fruit up to five inches wide follows in autumn. For fruit to ripen, pomegranates need full sun and a long, hot growing season. In cool climates, you can grow pomegranates in a greenhouse.

SPECIAL FEATURES: Funnel-shape flower with wrinkled orange-red petals; yellow-brown or yellow-red edible fruit.

HARDINESS: Zone 8.

LIGHT: Full sun to partial shade.

SOIL: Tolerates most well-drained soils. Plant in standard bonsai mix.

WATER: Daily during growth, sparingly in winter without letting the soil completely dry out.

FERTILIZER: Feed every two weeks with liquid fertilizer from spring to fall.

PRUNING: Pomegranate blooms on new growth. Prune new shoots to the first two pairs of leaves, retaining the smaller shoots tipped with round flower buds. Prune excess growth all summer.

REPOT: Every two years in early spring if necessary.

PESTS AND DISEASES: Scales, powdery mildew, and dieback.

STYLES: Multistemmed by nature, pomegranates adapt well to multitrunk styles such as clump, sinuous, and double- or triple-trunk. To make a single-curved, slanting, windswept, or literati style, you need to choose one strong stem and cut out the suckers around it. Avoid erect formal styles like straight-trunk and broom, which defy dwarf pomegranate's relaxed habit.

CULTIVARS AND VARIETIES: 'Nana', dense round shrub 1 to 3 feet high and wide with abundant fruit. Good for small bonsai.

The irregular charm of a fruiting *P. granatum* stands out in this informal-upright bonsai.

Quercus
KWAYR-kus

OAK
Fagaceae

Often grown for broad lobed leaves, rounded acorns, vast spreading limbs, and immense tapering trunks, oaks rank high among familiar landscape trees. In some species, deep crevices occur in the rough bark. Mature leaves may be bright yellow (*Q. robur* 'Concordia'), variegated (*Q. cerris* 'Argenteovariegata'), or in many shades of green. Fall color ranges from bright red (*Q. coccinea*) and orange (*Q. ×heterophylla*) to yellow and brown.

SPECIAL FEATURES: Majestic habit with widespread branching and grand tapering trunk; handsome leaves with superb fall color on some species.

HARDINESS: Zone 3, depending on the species, but always with protection from frost.

LIGHT: Full sun to partial shade.

SOIL: Moist, well-drained, fertile. Many tolerate some soil alkalinity. Plant in standard bonsai mix.

WATER: Check daily during the growing season to ensure the soil stays moist (not wet). Water less in winter without letting the soil go dry.

FERTILIZER: During summer and fall, feed every other week with balanced liquid fertilizer.

PRUNING: Cut back new grow to one or two leaves in spring and early summer

REPOT: Every one to three years, depending on the age and vigor of the tree. Release and lift tree from container to determine if the roots are crowded.

PESTS AND DISEASES: Galls, gypsy moths, borers, skeletonizers, leaf miners, mildews, anthracnose, wilt.

STYLES: Curved-trunk, slanting, broom, and all multitrunk styles including clump, group, and raft.

CULTIVARS AND SPECIES: *Q. dentata*, Daimyo oak, Japanese emperor oak, native to sunny thickets in eastern Asia; grows slowly up to 60 feet high; part of the white oak group

with large 10-inch, dark green leaves that turn brown in fall and often stay on the tree in winter; needs acid soil; Zone 6.

'Pinnatifida', skinny featherlike leaf lobes are finer textured than the species; slow growing.

Q. ilicifolia, scrub oak, petite spreading tree to 20 feet; red or yellow fall color; native to eastern United States; Zone 5.

Q. robur 'Concordia', English oak, small tree to 30 feet with luminous yellow leaves that change to green.

Q. suber, cork bark oak, Mediterranean native evergreen up to 70 feet high with outstanding corky bark used in commerce; deeply furrowed bark; popular for bonsai; full sun; Zone 7.

Q. virginiana, live oak, evergreen tree that is wider than tall; native to southern United States; Zone 8.

Pruning reduces the natural 10-inch leaves of Q. *dentata*, Daimyo oak, to a smaller size in keeping with a potted bonsai tree.

Rhododendron indicum hybrids
Roh-doh-DEN-dron IN-di-kum

SATSUKI AZALEA
Ericaceae

When Satsuki azaleas bloom, their lavish funnel-shape flowers hide the little evergreen leaves. Satsuki describes the bloom time (fifth month) of these flowering shrubs in their native Japan, when they produce abundant trusses of pink, red, purple, or white flowers. The Japanese have created countless *R. indicum* hybrids because its small foliage and diminutive spreading form lend themselves to bonsai and areas of limited space. Flowers vary from solid orange-red, pink, or lavender to multihued hybrids with colored dots, streaks, bands, and solid colors all on the same plant at the same time. While it flowers, shield your Satsuki from downpours. Heavy rain can damage the petals and decrease the bloom period.

SPECIAL FEATURES: Lavish flowers in tints of pink, red, white, or purple; sometimes striped, spotted, or rimmed with contrasting hues. Solid-colored blooms may appear on the same plants with variegated flowers.

Satsuki azalea in the slanting style attracts attention both for its showy pink flowers and for its exposed, contorted roots.

HARDINESS: Zone 7 with protection from frost.

■LIGHT: Partial shade to sun. The farther north you live, the more sun your azalea can tolerate.

SOIL: Like all rhododendrons, Satsuki azaleas thrive in moist, acid soil. Plant in acid bonsai mix.

WATER: Daily during the growing season. Decrease water in winter, but do not let azaleas dry out in cold weather. Mist leaves lightly in summer, especially in windy sites. Wetting leaves when the plant is in full sun may cause leaf scorch.

FERTILIZER: Start feeding every other week with soluble fertilizer for acid-loving plants early in the growing season. Pause while the shrub blooms, then resume monthly until fall.

PRUNING: Pinch wilted blooms after flowering. Prune new growth at the end of the bloom period. Trim some of the second flush until the middle of summer. Wire the plant in early summer after it flowers. Shape trees by pruning branches and wiring in early spring.

REPOT: If you want flowers every year, repot immediately after blooming every one to three years, although it may take the tree a while to recover from the process. Or you can repot in early spring before blooming to strengthen the plant. In that case, snip or rub off the flower buds before they open to help roots regain their vigor fast.

PESTS AND DISEASES: Aphids, whiteflies, scales, chlorosis.

STYLES: Satsuki azaleas suit most styles, especially curved-trunk, slanted, windswept, all multitrunk styles, cascade, semi-cascade, and root-over-rock.

CULTIVARS: 'Juko', small leaves and varied flowers on one shrub. Some blossoms have pale purplish pink petals with dark pink bands or dots; some are plain pink or rose with or without white margins.

The exposed woody roots of Satsuki azalea contribute to the twisted splendor of this curved-trunk bonsai tree.

'Rinpu', pink flower with dark pink flare, twisted leaves, grows up to 12 inches high, for *mame* and very small bonsai.

Kurume hybrids, crosses among *R. kiusianum*, *R. kaempferi*, and *R. obtusum*. Dwarfs with purple, red, pink, salmon, lavender, orange, white, or bicolor flowers; single and double petals. Many hybrids have hose-in-hose blooms with two flower tubes, one inside the other.

Schefflera arboricola
SHEF-ler-uh ar-bor-i-KOH-luh

ARBORICOLA, MINIATURE UMBRELLA PLANT
Araliaceae

Grown as a houseplant for its attractive handlike foliage, this tropical evergreen shrub grows more than 5 feet high in its native Taiwan. Schefflera remains popular because it is easy to cultivate and survives occasional neglect. Many people buy ready-made arboricola bonsai as an introduction to the art or to give as gifts. Its mature foliage differs from the juvenile toothed leaves. This slow-growing *Schefflera* sometimes produces aerial roots more advanced bonsai growers can use to advantage when styling.

SPECIAL FEATURES: Handsome evergreen foliage arranged like the palm of a hand. In tropical conditions, it bears red upright flower clusters at the branch tips and orange fruits that darken over time.

HARDINESS: Zone 9b. Grow outdoors when nighttime temperatures are above 60° F. You can also keep arboricola indoors year-round in a warm room out of direct sunlight.

LIGHT: Partial shade outdoors, bright indirect light indoors.

SOIL: Moist, well-drained soil outdoors. Prefers a little alkalinity. Plant in standard bonsai mix.

WATER: Every couple of days during the growing season to keep the soil from drying out. Water sparingly in winter—just enough to moisten the soil. Mist the plant occasionally and wipe leaves with a damp paper towel to keep them clean.

FERTILIZER: Monthly with liquid food during the growing season.

PRUNING: Pinch stems to promote branching and to create a dense, broad, rounded crown. Prune in early spring or late summer. Fleshy stems are difficult to wire.

REPOT: Every year in late winter or early spring. Arboricola roots are robust and can withstand drastic pruning when necessary.

PESTS AND DISEASES: Usually a healthy plant that can survive a little neglect. Occasional spider mites, scales, thrips, mealybugs.

STYLES: Curved-trunk, root-over-rock, coiled, and multitrunk styles are prevalent.

CULTIVARS AND SPECIES: S. actinophylla, Queensland umbrella tree, a big evergreen shrub or small tree grows up to 40 feet tall. It has red flowers in summer and dark, shiny, umbrellalike green leaves made up of 7 to 16 leaflets up to 12 inches long. Considered a self-sowing pest in Florida when grown outdoors, it also makes a successful and vigorous houseplant.

Set on a rock slab, this clump-style arboricola with its multiple trunks and tangled root mass looks like a small grove of trees.

Serissa foetida
Sub-RISS-uh FET-i-duh

JAPANESE SERISSA, TREE OF A THOUSAND STARS, SNOW ROSE
Rubiaceae

Serissa forms a low domed shrub suitable for groundcover in its native Southeast Asia. Grown mostly indoors in North America, it takes well to pruning and makes an excellent small to miniature bonsai. The foliage is usually tiny, shiny and dark green, although variegated forms exist. In summer plentiful pink buds open to white or pink, single or double blooms, depending on the variety. Although evergreen, the inner branches occasionally shed some leaves. Set the potted serissa on a humidity tray spread with a layer of damp gravel because this subtropical to tropical plant likes a humid environment. Misting the foliage may also help.

SPECIAL FEATURES: Tiny white or pink flowers and diminutive solid or variegated leaves.

HARDINESS: Zone 11. Place serissa outdoors when nighttime temperatures rise above 50° F. In autumn, bring indoors to a warm (over 65° F), brightly lit room to keep it growing, or overwinter it in a bright place at 45° F. Avoid setting it in drafts indoors and in windy spots outside. Leaf drop can be a problem.

LIGHT: Outdoors in full sun with some afternoon shade. Bright indirect light indoors.

SOIL: Moist, well-drained, fertile soil in the landscape. In containers, use standard bonsai mix.

WATER: Every day throughout the growing season. Needs little water in winter. Likes high humidity so set the container on a humidity tray with damp gravel and mist leaves when not blooming.

FERTILIZER: Twice a month with balanced liquid fertilizer from spring to fall and monthly thereafter.

PRUNING: Shape by clipping branches in late winter or after flowering. To wire serissa, proceed cautiously since branches are fragile. Trim new growth back to one or two sets of leaves after flowering.

REPOT: Every other year check roots in early spring; repot if needed.
PESTS AND DISEASES: Scales.
STYLES: Adapted to most styles except straight-trunk and broom.
CULTIVARS: 'Flore Pleno', double white flowers on smaller plant.

'Mt. Fuji', variegated green leaves with white margins, single white blooms, erect habit.

'Kyoto', dark green foliage, pink buds open to diminutive single white blooms, upright branching.

Serissa, grown indoors in much of North America, flowers in summer.

Taxodium distichum
Tak-SOH-dee-um DIS-tik-kum

BALD CYPRESS
Taxodiaceae

Bald cypress is native to the swamps of the southeastern United States, where it grows in groves. Around these drenched lowland trees, sections of root rise from the water, forming odd tapering projections know as cypress "knees." This fine-textured deciduous conifer has distinctive needlelike leaves that change from chartreuse in late spring to mossy green in summer and orange in fall. In the landscape, the tree has a slim, conical shape when young but the crown flattens with age. The flared, fluted trunk narrows steeply, growing up to 70 feet high. *Taxodium distichum* bonsai can recreate the tree's flared, tapering trunk in miniature.

SPECIAL FEATURES: Tapered, muscular trunk with flared base; gray stringy bark splotched orange; orange-bronze fall color; produces "knees" in wet conditions.

HARDINESS: Zone 5 with protection.

LIGHT: Full sun.

SOIL: Moist to wet acid soil; withstands wind and salt. Plant in an acid bonsai mix.

WATER: Ample water although established landscape trees can tolerate some drought. Check bonsai daily during the growing season.

FERTILIZER: Feed with fertilizer formulated for acid-loving plants since soils with a high pH can turn the leaves yellow (chlorosis).

PRUNING: Trim branches in early spring before growth begins or in fall. Cut back shoots and leaves in early summer. Leaf cutting can reduce the size of the foliage. Shape bald cypress by wiring in early spring or midsummer.

REPOT: Every year or two, depending on the age and vigor of the tree.

PESTS AND DISEASES: Mites, moths, wood rot.

STYLES: Its straight trunk and vigorous growth are particularly suited to the straight-trunk style, which emulates bald cypress's youthful shape. Many bonsai artists on the U.S. Gulf Coast work in a nontraditional "flat top" style that represents bald cypress's mature form as it grows in the wild. *Taxodium* makes a fine large bonsai.

This bald cypress bonsai displays the erect habit and flaring tapered trunk typical of the species.

Taxus baccata
TAK-sus buk-KAH-ta

ENGLISH OR COMMON YEW
Taxaceae

In addition to hedging, yews also make excellent bonsai. These vigorous evergreen conifers grow in sun and shade. They tolerate severe pruning and develop leaves on old and new wood. The needled foliage is glossy dark green on top, lighter green below. English yew is by nature a conical tree with broad horizontal limbs and exfoliating, purplish brown bark. Male plants produce yellow cones in spring while females bear decorative ½-inch red fruits enclosing one green seed in fall. Only the juicy red protective coat surrounding the seed is edible. The rest of the plant is poisonous. If you want berries on a female yew, grow a male nearby to pollinate it. Nurseries offer cultivars in varying colors and sizes.

SPECIAL FEATURES: Adaptable conifer with flat blackish green needles and poisonous seeds in red fleshy coats.

HARDINESS: Zone 6, with winter protection for bonsai.

LIGHT: Full sun to deep shade when planted in the ground. Keep bonsai in light to deep shade.

SOIL: Well-drained soil, pH tolerant.

WATER: Water every day from spring to fall. In winter give it just enough water to keep the soil from drying out. Too much and too little water can kill it.

FERTILIZER: Feed every two weeks from spring to fall with a balanced liquid fertilizer.

PRUNING: Pinch fresh shoots to ½ inch through the growing season. Shape by trimming branches and wiring in the fall.

REPOT: Every two years in early spring, check the roots of your yew and repot it when necessary.

Yew bonsai can tolerate shady, polluted, and coastal sites.

PESTS AND DISEASES: Deer, scales, mealybug, black vine weevil.

STYLES: Except for broom, all styles including curved-suspended and straight-trunk.

CULTIVARS AND SPECIES: *T. cuspidata*, Japanese yew, slow-growing; hardy to Zone 4; use *T. c.* 'Nana', a dwarf, for little bonsai.

Tsuga diversifolia
SU-gah di-ver-si-FOH-lee-ah

JAPANESE HEMLOCK
Pinaceae

A hemlock lives in sun or shade. A droopy central leader caps its conical form. Branch tips also dangle, giving the tree a graceful appearance. Flat needlelike leaves ¼ to ½ inch long have dark green tops and white-striped bottoms. Overall, the tree's texture appears soft and shaggy. Male and female parts coexist on the same tree, but the small hanging female cones are not particularly ornamental.

SPECIAL FEATURES: Short, shiny, dark green needled leaves give trees a wispy aspect; orange shoots and orange-brown bark.

HARDINESS: Zone 5.

LIGHT: Sun to shade. Partial shade is ideal for bonsai. Plant in standard bonsai mix.

SOIL: In the landscape, Japanese hemlock likes moist, well-drained soil high in organic matter.

WATER: Every day from spring to fall, less during the winter; soil should not dry out completely.

FERTILIZER: Every other week with liquid fertilizer from spring to fall.

PRUNING: Hemlock does not sprout on old wood. Be careful when pruning to leave some new wood where you want new growth to sprout. Prune branches any time of year. Pinch back fresh shoots with thumb and forefinger during the summer. Wire when tree is not in active growth.

REPOT: Hemlock, which has fibrous roots, needs repotting every two years in early spring.

PESTS AND DISEASES: Wooly adelgid, scale, and mites.

STYLES: Hemlock is versatile. Train it in any style except broom.

CULTIVARS AND SPECIES:
T. canadensis, Canadian hemlock, eastern North American native with ridged gray bark; 'Verkade's Recurved', contorted needles and branchlets on 3-foot dwarf; Zone 4.

T. heterophylla, Western hemlock, western North American native with purplish brown bark; Zone 6.

Foliage pads on upper branches expose the graceful, subtly curved trunk of T. diversifolia.

Ulmus parvifolia
UL-mus par-vi-FOH-lee-uh

LACEBARK ELM
Ulmaceae

Small leaves, ornamental bark, and a strong pattern of growth make lacebark elm a bonsai classic. In nature, this handsome semi-evergreen or deciduous tree grows up to 50 feet high and wide. It tolerates most soil and atmospheric conditions including air pollution. Lacebark's leaves, ¾ to 2½ inches long, are tiny compared with many other elm species. Its dense display of twigs goes well with the round-topped broom style. If you grow lacebark elm bonsai indoors or in a warm climate, the foliage stays green all year. Grown outdoors in cool climates, however, *U. parvifolia* is deciduous. Protect it from frost damage by setting it in a garage or shed in the fall.

SPECIAL FEATURES: Shiny, deep green foliage with serrated edges, fine twiggy branches; peeling outer bark exposing orange, green, and grayish brown blotches.

HARDINESS: Zone 4 or 5 with winter protection for bonsai below 23° F.

LIGHT: Sun to partial shade.

SOIL: Survives in most well-drained soils. Plant in standard bonsai mix.

WATER: Check elms grown outdoors at least once a day in summer for watering. During winter dormancy, water outdoor elms before they dry out. Indoor evergreen elms will need more winter watering than those grown outdoors.

FERTILIZER: Feed every week during the growing season and every month in winter when grown indoors. For outdoor trees, feed every other week with balanced liquid fertilizer beginning when the tree leafs out and continuing to summer's end.

PRUNING: Trim branches in spring before seasonal growth begins. Prune shoots back to one or two leaves in late spring.

REPOT: Every one to three years before bud break, depending upon the maturity and variety of the tree.

PESTS AND DISEASES: Healthy specimens resist most elm pests.

STYLES: All bonsai sizes and styles, including straight-trunk, slanting, group planting, and broom styles.

CULTIVARS AND SPECIES: 'Frosty' has white-edged leaves shorter than 1 inch. It grows slowly to 20 feet tall.

'Hokkaido', princess elm, dwarf with minute ⅛ inch foliage, corky bark, grows to 3×3 feet.

U. ×hollandica 'Jacqueline Hillier', leafy, shrubby and slow growing to 6×8 feet.

Exfoliating bark and an outstanding pattern of ramification give lacebark elm, a deciduous tree, an outstanding winter form.

Zelkova serrata
Zel-KOH-vah ser-RAY-tah

JAPANESE GRAY-BARK ELM, JAPANESE ZELKOVA
Ulmaceae

Gray-bark elm, which grows up to 80 feet high, is valued for its straight trunk; pleasing vase-shape symmetry; red, orange, or yellow fall color; and gray bark that changes with age.

Younger trees have smooth gray bark with noticeable striations known as lenticils. The bark of older trees is gray and slightly peeling to expose areas of orange-gray.

Because zelkova resembles American elm but resists Dutch elm disease, it is a popular elm substitute along city streets. Its outstanding branching pattern makes it an excellent subject for deciduous bonsai. The broom style takes advantage of zelkova's upright form, ascending branches, and dainty crowded twigs. With care you can use this vigorous, relatively small-leafed tree for any bonsai style.

SPECIAL FEATURES: Erect habit, glowing fall color, beautiful bark.

HARDINESS: Zone 4 or 5, depending upon the cultivar. Zelkova needs winter protection.

LIGHT: Sun year-round except for the heat of summer, when it needs partial shade.

SOIL: Moist, well-drained soil is ideal. Plant in standard bonsai mix.

WATER: Once a day during the growing season. Do not let soil dry out in winter.

FERTILIZER: Every other week during the growing season.

PRUNING: To enhance branching, keep pinching young shoots to two sets of leaves in late spring and early summer. Shape by directional pruning in early spring or fall.

REPOT: Every one to five years in spring, with fast-growing young trees needing more frequent repotting.

PESTS AND DISEASES: Better disease resistance than other elms. Some spider mites on bonsai.

STYLES: Most styles will work, especially broom.

CULTIVARS: 'Goblin', dwarf 4×4-foot bush for very small bonsai.

'Green Vase', dynamic, vaselike plant with limbs forming upright, elegant arcs. Good for medium to large bonsai.

The massed trunks of Japanese gray-bark elm display its luminous fall color to advantage.

Glossary

BANKAN: (Coiled-trunk style) Tree with a spiraling trunk.

BONSAI: Literally, a tree in a tray or pot; the art and skill of miniaturizing a tree that imitates nature in a container.

BUNJIN-GI: (Literati style) Elegant tree with a slender, slanting, elongated trunk and short, delicate branches toward the top. Planted in a small round or octagonal pot.

CHOKKAN: (Straight-trunk, formal-upright style) Trees in this style have an upright trunk and a balanced crown with well-spaced branches. The trunk, rising from large roots that spread in every direction, tapers from the base to the crown.

FUKINAGASHI: (Windswept) Trees are similar to those in the slanting style, but all limbs sweep in one direction as if the tree were growing where a constant wind whips the tree.

GOKAN: (five-trunk) Usually one trunk is the largest and is referred to as the "parent."

HOKIDACHI: (Broom) Broom-style trees have upright trunks with symmetrical fanlike crowns, like the shape of an upside-down broom.

IKADABUKI: (Raft style) Tree created by laying a live trunk, branch, or root on the ground. A line of shoots emerges from the horizontal base and matures into a row of tree trunks.

ISHIZUKI OR ISHITSUKI: (Rock-grown styles) Rock-grown bonsai trees symbolize the harshness of nature. They develop over the top of or in soil-packed clefts of specially chosen irregular stones. In Sekijojuk, root-over-rock, the upper part of the roots grip the rock while the base is planted in the soil from which the rock emerges.

JIN: A deadwood technique simulating either a dead branch stub or a dead treetop in order to make a tree look older.

KABUDACHI: (Clump, multiple-trunks) Good conformation is based on the aesthetic balance of the smaller "children" to the parent in trunk thickness.

KENGAI: (Cascade style) The tree trunk and branches bend over the edge of the pot as if the tree were pulled by its own weight. The branches grow below the bottom of the bonsai dish, which is small at the rim and deep to balance the tree form. *Han-kengai* (semi-cascade) is similar to the cascade, except that the tree looks more horizontal and branches do not extend below the bottom of the pot, which is shallower than that of the cascade.

MAME: Miniature bonsai standing 2 to 6 inches tall.

MYO-GI: (Curved-trunk, informal-upright style) Erect tree with a full balanced crown and a single gently curving trunk that tapers toward the top.

NEAGARI: (Raised or exposed root) Woody roots protrude upwards from the ground, so the ravaged-looking trunk appears to float in the air.

NEBARI: The exposed root structure of a bonsai tree. A good nebari balances the visual weight of the crown and creates an aged, weathered appearance.

NETSURANARI OR NETSUNAGARI: (Sinuous or root-linked style) Sinuous bonsai have multiple trees growing from a single sinuous root, as in nature some trees produce lesser trees at random from the roots.

SABAMIKI: A deadwood style in which part of the tree trunk is hollowed to create an appearance of great age.

SAIKEI: A tray landscape representing entire scenes from nature.

SANKAN: (Triple-trunk style) Three trunks growing from the same root.

SHAKAN: (Slanting) Trees in the slanting style have single trunks and grow straight toward the crown but at a sloping angle.

SHARI: A deadwood technique that deadens part of a tree trunk.

SHARIMIKI: The driftwood technique deadens all but a few stripes of live bark supporting a few live branches on the tree.

SHOHAKU: The Japanese put most evergreens into the shohaku bonsai group, a category that includes the classic pine bonsai.

SOKAN: (Twin-trunk style) Two trunks growing from the same root.

YOSE-UE: (Group planting) Group plantings represent trees in any situation such as an orchard or forest where a large number of trees grow together in the landscape. Group plantings combine individual trees, each grown on its own roots.

ZOKI: Trees that do not belong to the traditional shohaku bonsai group, which includes most deciduous trees.

Symmetrical branch pads on *Rhododendron eriocarpum* 'Eikan', a bonsai in the curved-trunk style, give the tree a sense of equilibrium and formality.

USDA Plant Hardiness Zone Map

This map of climate zones helps you select plants for your garden that will survive a typical winter in your region. The United States Department of Agriculture (USDA) developed the map, basing the zones on the lowest recorded temperatures across North America. Zone 1 is the coldest area and Zone 11 is the warmest one.

Plants are classified by the coldest temperature and zone they can endure. For example, plants hardy to Zone 6 survive where winter temperatures drop to –10°F. Those hardy to Zone 8 die long before it is that cold. These plants may grow in colder regions but must be replaced each year. Plants rated for a range of hardiness zones can usually survive winter in the coldest region as well as tolerate the summer heat of the warmest.

To find your hardiness zone, note the approximate location of your community on the map; then match the color band marking that area to the key. Note that colder or hotter microclimates may exist in your garden.

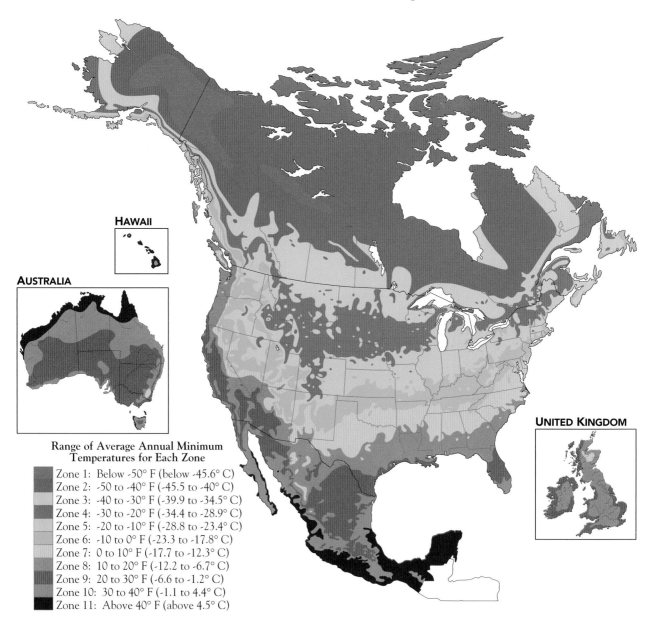

HAWAII

AUSTRALIA

UNITED KINGDOM

Range of Average Annual Minimum Temperatures for Each Zone

Zone 1: Below -50° F (below -45.6° C)
Zone 2: -50 to -40° F (-45.5 to -40° C)
Zone 3: -40 to -30° F (-39.9 to -34.5° C)
Zone 4: -30 to -20° F (-34.4 to -28.9° C)
Zone 5: -20 to -10° F (-28.8 to -23.4° C)
Zone 6: -10 to 0° F (-23.3 to -17.8° C)
Zone 7: 0 to 10° F (-17.7 to -12.3° C)
Zone 8: 10 to 20° F (-12.2 to -6.7° C)
Zone 9: 20 to 30° F (-6.6 to -1.2° C)
Zone 10: 30 to 40° F (-1.1 to 4.4° C)
Zone 11: Above 40° F (above 4.5° C)

Resources

Plants by mail order or Internet

Brussels Bonsai Nursery, LLC
8365 Center Hill Rd.
Olive Branch, MS 38654
800/582-2593
www.brusselsbonsai.com
Trees and supplies

Cape Cod Bonsai Studio
1012 Rte. 28
Harwich, MA 02645
508/432-8400
www.capecodbonsai.com
Trees and supplies

Cascade Bonsai Works
28137 Liberty Rd.
Sweet Home, OR 97386
541/367-4387
www.cascadebonsai.com
Plants and tools

Elandan Gardens
3050 W. State Hwy. 16
Bremerton, WA 98312
360/373-8260
www.elandangardens.com
Bonsai plants and supplies

Evergreen Gardenworks
P.O. Box 537
Kelseyville, CA 95451
www.evergreengardenworks.com
bonsai@pacific.net
Rare and unusual bonsai
    plants

Golden Arrow Bonsai
HC 73, Box 1742
Deadwood, SD 57732
605/342-4467
www.goldenarrowbonsai.com
Plants

Jiu-San Bonsai
1243 Melville Rd.
Farmingdale, NY 11535
631/293-9246
www.jiusanbonsai.com
Rare plants, containers,
    supplies and tools

Living Art Bonsai
1154 Barrow St.
Houma, LA 70360
866/926-6724
www.livingartbonsai.com
Specialists in Trident maples

Meehan's Bonsai Nursery
4925 Woodstock Lane
Rohrersville, MD 21779
301/432-2965
Supplies and unusual plants

Mendocino Coast Bonsai
P.O. Box 317
Point Arena, CA 95468
707/884-4126
www.mcbonsai.com
Specialists in redwoods, live
    oaks and cypress

Miami Tropical Bonsai
14775 SW 232 St.
Miami, FL 33170
800/777-0027
www.miamitropicalbonsai.com
Subtropical and tropical
    bonsai plants

Mountain Maples
54561 Registered Guest Rd.
P.O. Box 1329
Laytonville, CA 95454-1329
888/707-6522
www.mountainmaples.com
Japanese maple specialists

New England Bonsai Gardens
914 S. Main St.
Bellingham, MA 02019
800/845-0456
www.nebonsai.com
Plants and supplies

Nee-Hai Bonsai
3236 W. Ashlan
Fresno, CA 93722
559/221-0281
www.neehaibonsai.com
Plants, pots, and tools

The Potted Forest
37650 Farr Rd.
Dade City, FL 33523
352/518-1109
www.pottedforest.com
Bonsai and rare plants

Rare Find Nursery
957 Patterson Rd.
Jackson, NJ 08527
732/833-0613
www.rarefindnursery.com
Rhododendrons, Japanese
    maples, and other trees

Shanti Bithi Nursery, Inc.
3047 High Ridge Rd.
Stamford, CT 06903
203/329-0768
www.shantibithi.com
Plants, tools and supplies

Yasukunai Bonsai Garden
6061 Dempster
Morton Grove, IL 60053
847/966-5142
www.yasukunai.com
Plants and supplies

Asymmetric balance prevails in a *Pinus thunbergii* 'Conticosa' bonsai in the twin-trunk style.

Resources
(continued)

Bonsai supplies by mail order or Internet

Bonsai by the Monastery
2625 Hwy. 212 SW
Conyers, GA 30094
800/778-7687
www.bonsaimonk.com
Bonsai pots

Bonsai of Brooklyn
2418 McDonald Ave.
Brooklyn, NY 11223
917/325-3954
www.bonsaiofbrooklyn.com
Bonsai trees, tools and
   supplies

Bonsai Learning Center
4416 Beattie's Ford Rd.
Charlotte, NC 28216
704/392-9244
www.bonsailearningcenter.com
Tools and supplies

Dallas Bonsai Garden
4460 W. Walnut St., Suite 218
Garland, TX 75042
800/982-1223
(1-5 pm M-F CST)
www.dallasbonsai.com
Bonsai tools and supplies

DaSu Bonsai Studio
27877 Timber Rd.
Kelley, IA 50134
800/528-2827
www.bonsaitrees.com
Supplies and tools

DripWorks
190 Sanhedrin Circle
Willits, CA 95490
800/522-3747
www.dripworksusa.com
Bonsai watering systems

Ichiban Bonsai Products
8414 Brakeman Rd.
Chardon, OH 44024
440/285-2470
www.ichibanbonsai.com

Joshua Roth Limited
800/624-4635
www.joshuaroth.com
Bonsai tool specialists

Bonsai growing information and websites

Bonsai4Me
www.bonsai4me.com
Bonsai artist Harry
   Harrington's website
   containing bonsai
   techniques, species, and
   images

The Bonsai Primer
www.bonsaiprimer.com
Website of English bonsai
   artist Allen C. Roffey

Bonsai Web
www.bonsaiweb.com
Resource for tools, supplies,
   and tree care information

Evergreen Gardenworks
www.evergreengardenworks.com
   Information-packed website
   maintained by experienced
   bonsai growers living three
   hours north of San
   Francisco.
P.O. Box 537
Kelseyville, CA 95451

International Bonsai
Publishes *International
   Bonsai* magazine
P.O. Box 23894
Rochester, NY 14692
716/334-2595

Internet Bonsai Club
To subscribe, send email to:
   listserv@home.ease.lsoft.com.
   Write SUBSCRIBE BONSAI
   and your e-mail name in
   the text area.

Rosade Bonsai Studio
www.rosadebonsai.com
Bonsai links plus class
   information
6912 Ely Rd. – Solebury
New Hope, PA 18938-9634
215/862-5925

Stone Lantern Publishing Co.
www.stonelantern.com
Publishes *Bonsai Today*
   magazine
P.O. Box 324
Watertown, MA 02471
800/776-1167

Organizations

The American Bonsai Society
www.absbonsai.org
Covers North America
   including Mexico, the
   United States, and Canada
Publishes *Bonsai: Journal of
   the American Bonsai
   Society*
Offers Basic Bonsai
   Correspondence Course:
   Bonsai Instruction the
   Western Way
c/o ABS Executive Secretary
P. O. Box 351604
Toledo, OH 43635-1604,
   U.S.A.

Bonsai Clubs International
www.bonsai-bci.com
Publishes *Bonsai Magazine*

National Bonsai Foundation
The United States National
   Arboretum
www.bonsai-nbf.org
Visiting hours: 10 am to 3:30
   pm daily except Dec. 25
3501 New York Ave. N.E.
Washington D.C. 20002-1958
202/245-2726

Bonsai collections

The Arnold Arboretum of
  Harvard University
Fifteen trees from the Larz
  Anderson collection
On view from mid-April to the
  end of October
125 Arborway
Jamaica Plain, MA 02130-3500
617/524-1718
www.arboretum.harvard.edu

Brooklyn Botanical Garden
1000 Washington Ave.
Brooklyn, NY 11225
718/623 7200
www.bbg.org

Chicago Botanical Gardens
1000 Lake Cook Rd.
Glencoe, Illinois 60022
847/835-5440
www.chicagobotanic.org

Des Moines Botanical Center
905 East River Dr.
Des Moines, IA 50316-2897
515/242-2934

Fuku-Bonsai Cultural Center
  & Hawaii State Bonsai
  Repository
P.O. Box 6000 (Olaa Rd.)
Kurtistown, HI 96760
808/982-9880,
www.fukubonsai.com

Longwood Gardens
Fifteen of the 40 evergreen
  and deciduous specimens
  in the collection usually on
  display in the conservatory
Rte. 1
Kennett Square, PA 19348-0501
610/388-1000
www.longwoodgardens.org

Morikami Museum and
  Japanese Garden
4000 Morikami Park Rd.
Delray Beach, FL 33446
561/495-0233
  www.morikami.org

The National Bonsai and
  Penjing Museum
(Includes hardy and tropical
  specimens and a bonsai by
  American bonsai master,
  John Naka)
Visiting hours: 10 am to 3:30
  pm daily except Dec. 25
www.bonsai-nbf.org
The United States National
  Arboretum
3501 New York Ave. NE
Washington D.C. 20002-1958
202/245-2726

Northern California Bonsai
  Collection
Golden State Bonsai
  Collection-North
666 Bellevue Avenue
Lake Merritt
Oakland, CA 94602
510/797-4727

Southern California Bonsai
  Collection
Huntington Library, Art
  Collections, and Botanical
  Gardens
1151 Oxford Rd.
San Marino, CA 91108
625/405-2100
www.huntington.org

Index

METRIC CONVERSIONS

U.S. Units to Metric Equivalents			Metric Units to U.S. Equivalents		
To Convert From	**Multiply By**	**To Get**	**To Convert From**	**Multiply By**	**To Get**
Inches	25.4	Millimeters	Millimeters	0.0394	Inches
Inches	2.54	Centimeters	Centimeters	0.3937	Inches
Feet	30.48	Centimeters	Centimeters	0.0328	Feet
Feet	0.3048	Meters	Meters	3.2808	Feet
Yards	0.9144	Meters	Meters	1.0936	Yards
Square inches	6.4516	Square centimeters	Square centimeters	0.1550	Square inches
Square feet	0.0929	Square meters	Square meters	10.764	Square feet
Square yards	0.8361	Square meters	Square meters	1.1960	Square yards
Acres	0.4047	Hectares	Hectares	2.4711	Acres
Cubic inches	16.387	Cubic centimeters	Cubic centimeters	0.0610	Cubic inches
Cubic feet	0.0283	Cubic meters	Cubic meters	35.315	Cubic feet
Cubic feet	28.316	Liters	Liters	0.0353	Cubic feet
Cubic yards	0.7646	Cubic meters	Cubic meters	1.308	Cubic yards
Cubic yards	764.55	Liters	Liters	0.0013	Cubic yards

To convert from degrees Fahrenheit (F) to degrees Celsius (C), first subtract 32, then multiply by ⁵⁄₉.

To convert from degrees Celsius to degrees Fahrenheit, multiply by ⁹⁄₅, then add 32.